PRAISE FOR
SPEAKING FOR GOD

"Pam Barnett is undeniably knowledgeable regarding the subject matter. This book is sorely needed. I think it will really fill a gap in current Christian publishing. It is a fine book."

–Dr. Cal Easterling, Oral Roberts University senior professor and ordained minister

"A wealth of information! Thorough, important, and necessary. Tremendous stuff that will bless many."

–Eddie Smith, co-founder and executive director U.S. Prayer Center, owner/CEO Worldwide Publishing Group

"A superb work! Very impressive. Clear and thorough. One of the best resources ever of public speaking for Bible colleges and seminaries. It can serve as a book of reference and instruction for many years. Any serious speaker for God would benefit from reading this book. Lots of clear examples. A wealth of information. Everything just makes sense."

–Cecilie Croissant, MA, LPC, former director and teacher at the School of Worship at Victory Bible College; international conference speaker

"Excellent handbook for preachers! Lots of practical tips and spiritual insight into preaching. This book is a great tool for every preacher (experienced or inexperienced) to deliver God's messages in a more excellent way. This is a 'must have' book for every preacher."

–Amani Fam, missionary evangelist, Assemblies of God

SPEAKING *for* GOD

SPEAKING *for* GOD

*How to Preach and Speak
with Power, Passion, and Purpose*

PAM BARNETT

SPRINGS OF WATER PUBLICATIONS

Copyright © 2022 by Pam Barnett

All rights reserved. No portion of this book may be reproduced, stored in a retrieval system, or transmitted in any form or by any means—electronic, mechanical, photocopy, recording, scanning, or other—except for brief quotations in critical reviews or articles, without the prior written permission of the publisher.

SPEAKING FOR GOD:
How to Preach and Speak with Power, Passion, and Purpose

ISBN 978-1-7361760-0-9 (paperback)
ISBN 978-1-7361760-1-6 (ebook)
Library of Congress Control Number: 2020923182

Published by Springs of Water Publications, PO Box 664, Thomaston, GA 30286
SpeakingForGod.com
Email: speakingforgod@cfaith.com

All Scripture quotations are from the Authorized King James Version of the Holy Bible. Bolded text in Scripture quotations are the author's own emphasis.

Cover photo: Colourbox.com / Mykola Mazuryk
Cover and interior design: KUHN Design Group

Some content taken from *Expository Preaching with Word Pictures* by Jack Hughes. Used by permission of Christian Focus Publications, Scotland. Copyright © 2001.

Some content taken from *The Elements of Preaching* by Warren Wiersbe and David Wiersbe. Copyright © 1986. Used by permission of Tyndale House Publishers, Inc. All rights reserved.

Some content taken from *The Anatomy of Preaching: Identifying the Issues in Preaching Today* © Copyright 1989 by David L. Larsen. Published by Kregel Publications, Grand Rapids, MI. Used by permission of the publisher. All rights reserved.

Publisher's Cataloging-In-Publication Data

Names: Barnett, Pam, author.
Title: Speaking for God : how to preach and speak with power, passion, and purpose / Pam Barnett.
Description: Thomaston, GA : Springs of Water Publications, [2022] | Includes bibliographical references.
Identifiers: ISBN 9781736176009 (paperback) | ISBN 9781736176016 (ebook)
Subjects: LCSH: Preaching. | Church work. | Public speaking.
Classification: LCC BV4211.3 .B37 2022 (print) | LCC BV4211.3 (ebook) | DDC 251--dc23

This book is dedicated:

*To every person
who has ever wanted
to be loved*

and

*To every preacher and speaker
who ever has or ever will
step up and speak for God.*

PRAYER OF DEDICATION

One morning in the fifth month of writing this book, I woke up praying this prayer.

Build Your book, Lord,

To build Your preachers,

To build Your people,

To build Your kingdom,

That Your will may be done on this earth,

That all may come to an acknowledging of the truth,

That none would perish.

Oh God, save the people!

May they all come into Your family.

Thank You for using me, Father.

I appreciate the assignment.

Glory be to Your holy name forever.

Amen

CONTENTS

Acknowledgments xv
Introduction xvii

SECTION I: Foundational Information for the Preacher 1

Chapter 1: Preaching Basics 3
   What Is Preaching? 5
   Why Do We Preach? 5
   What Is the Goal of Preaching? 6
   What Is Most Important When You Preach? 7
   Why Should a Preacher Learn Public-Speaking Skills? 7

Chapter 2: Preaching Is a Relationship Event 9

Chapter 3: How to Connect With the Audience 13
   Meet the Needs of the Audience 13
   Show the Audience You Care About Them 15
   Share Something of Yourself With the Audience 17
   Share Something You Have Noticed About Them 18
   Audience Involvement Techniques 19
   More Ways to Connect With and Relate to the Audience 25

Chapter 4: How to Build Credibility as a Preacher 27
   What Is a Credibility Gap? 27
   How People Determine Your Credibility 27
   How to Develop Credibility 28
   Live a Life of Integrity 28
   Stay Away From Pride 30
   Help People Trust You 31
   More Ways to Build Credibility 33

Chapter 5: Guidelines for a Guest Speaker or Traveling Minister . . . 35

Chapter 6: The Anointing 39
- What Is the Anointing? 39
- Anointed for a Certain Office 40
- The Situational Anointing: The Intensified Power and Presence of God 42
- The Anointing Is Not Limited to Any Denomination or Preaching Style 43
- Jesus Needed the Anointing and So Do We 43
- What Blocks the Anointing? 44
- Positioning Ourselves for the Anointing 46

Chapter 7: What Is the Gospel? 51
- What Is the Gospel? 53
- Announcing the Good News of Salvation Through Jesus Christ 54
- Four-Point Gospel Message 56

SECTION II: How to Overcome Fear of Preaching 61
- Introduction 63

Chapter 8: Stage Fright 65

Chapter 9: The Before-Speaking Routine 67
- Physical Warm-Ups 68
- Vocal Warm-Ups 70
- Abdominal Breathing 73
- Bathroom Break 74
- Appearance Check 74

Chapter 10: Fear-Reduction Techniques 75
- #1 Pray and Dedicate Your Message to God 76
- #2 Know Your Message 76
- #3 Warm Up Your Body and Voice 76
- #4 Learn Basic Information on Fear of Public Speaking 76
- #5 Identify Your Fears 77

    #6 Monitor Your Self-Talk 79
    #7 Choose Your Attitudes 79
    #8 Get Up to Share 81
    #9 Identify How Your Message Will Help People 81
    #10 Let Go of Perfectionism 81
    #11 Watch Out for Assumptions 82
    #12 Pretend You Are Answering a Question 83
    #13 Think About the People, Their Needs, and God's Answer
          to Those Needs 83
    #14 Praise God 84
    #15 Use Spiritual Weapons 84
    #16 Find Scripture That Will Strengthen You 85
    #17 See People Through God's Eyes 85
    #18 Breathe Deeply and Speak Your Faith 86
    #19 Accept God's Love: Perfect Love Casts Out Fear 87
    #20 Be Bold 87
    #21 Trust God 88

Chapter 11: How to Manage Fear Symptoms During the Message . . . 89

Chapter 12: Confidence and the Perception of Confidence 93
    How Does a Speaker Develop Confidence? 93
    The Perception of Confidence 94
    Reasons for Authentic Confidence 95

SECTION III: Long-Term Preparation 97
    Introduction 99

Chapter 13: Take Care of the Temple of God 101
    Nutrition 101
    Sleep 103
    Exercise 103
    Forgiveness 103

Casting Your Cares on the Lord 103
Being Led by the Spirit of God 104

Chapter 14: Preliminary Research 107
Interview the Meeting Planner 107
Verify the Agreement in Writing 109

Chapter 15: Identify Your Habits 111
Physical Habits 111
Vocal Habits 112
Emotional Habits 112

Chapter 16: Prayers Before Preaching 115
Relationship With God 116
Fasting and Prayer 116
Intercessory Prayers 116
Praying Scripture Over Yourself 117
Holy Spirit-Written Prayers 118
Praying Aloud in the Pulpit at the Beginning of the Message 118

SECTION IV: Writing the Message 121
Introduction 123

Chapter 17: Follow Basic Message Guidelines 125
#1 Write Simple, Well-Organized Messages 125
#2 Make the Message Scriptural 125
#3 Meet People's Needs 127
#4 Demonstrate the Need 127
#5 Explain the Benefits of Applying the Message 127
#6 Explain How to Apply the Message 128
#7 Speak From Your Heart 129
#8 Point Out That the Bible Is God's Love Letter to Humans 129
#9 Keep in Mind Your Purpose 130
#10 Include a Call for Action 130

Chapter 18: Choose the Message 131
   How Can You Discover What to Preach? . . . 132
   Bible Lectures vs. Bible Messages 134
   Keep Your Goal in Mind 134

Chapter 19: Organize the Message, Part I 135
   How to Organize a Message 135
   Prayer 135
   Purpose 136
   The Three Parts of a Speech 137
   Transitions 146

Chapter 20: Organize the Message, Part II 149
   How to Create an Outline 149
   How to Shorten or Lengthen the Message . . 153
   The Sure-Fire Success Formula 154
   Holy Spirit-Led Preparation 154

Chapter 21: Choose the Right Words: General Guidelines 155
   Simplicity 155
   Sentence Length 156
   Abbreviations 156
   Jargon 156
   Slang 156
   Sarcasm 157
   Insults 157
   Humor 158
   Cultural Sayings and Idioms 158
   Definitions and Explanations 158
   The Discretionary Rule for What *Not* to Include in Your Message . . . 159
   Prejudice and Offensive Labels 159
   The Sanctity of the Pulpit 160

Chapter 22: Use Imagery to Anchor a Concept 161
   Metaphors, Similes, and Other Analogies . . . 162

  Anecdotes 165

  Testimonies 167

  Stories 168

  Generalized Personal Experiences 169

  Dialogue 169

  Illustrations 170

  Statement of Human Behavior 170

  Examples 171

  Imagery Related to the Listeners' Lifestyle 171

Chapter 23: Create Memorable Wording 173

  Alliteration 173

  Repetition 174

  Rule of Three 174

  Parallel Structure 175

  Opposites 176

  Rhymes 178

  Preparatory Statements 179

  Adaptation of a Well-Known Saying 179

  Combinations of Word-Crafting Tools 179

SECTION V: Short-Term Preparation 181

Chapter 24: The Week Before the Message 183

  Follow Clothing and Appearance Guidelines 183

  Organize Supplies 184

  Become Familiar With the Location 185

  Arrange the Seating 186

  Finish Your Preparation on the Day of the Message 187

Chapter 25: Five Ways to Deliver a Message 189

  Speak From Note Cards or an Outline 189

  Memorize Main Ideas and Speak Extemporaneously 190

  Speak Impromptu 190

    Memorize a Word-for-Word Manuscript 190
    Read a Word-for-Word Manuscript 191

Chapter 26: How to Practice Delivery of the Message 193
    How to Practice the Message 193
    Practice Yielding to the Inspirational Holy Spirit Flow 195

SECTION VI: Delivering the Message 197
    Introduction: Delivery Goals 199

Chapter 27: Evaluate Your Readiness to Preach 201

Chapter 28: Grammar and Pronunciation Guidelines 203

Chapter 29: Vocal Patterns While Preaching 207
    Basic Speaking Instruction Regarding Vocal Patterns 207
    How Your Anointing May Affect Your Vocal Pattern 208
    How to Use Vocal Variety 209
    How to Avoid Voice Misuse and Voice Abuse 213
    How to Read Scripture Aloud 215

Chapter 30: How to Use Your Body During the Message 217
    Physical Suggestions 217
    Movement and Gestures 218
    What to Do With Your Hands When You Preach 220

Chapter 31: Beginning the Message: What to Do in the First Minute . . 221

Chapter 32: How to Handle the Microphone 223
    Types of Microphones 223
    Tips for Using a Microphone 225

Chapter 33: Presentation Modifications for Specific Groups 227
    Preaching With an Interpreter 227
    Help People Understand Your Dialect 228
    Preaching to Children or to a Youth Group 228
    Preaching to the Elderly 229

Chapter 34: How to Give Altar Calls 231
    Two Types of Altar Calls 232
    Additional Details 234
    Repeat-After-Me Prayers 234
    Salvation Prayers 235
    Prayer for Application of the Message 236

Chapter 35: Finish-Up Details After You Preach 237
    Questions to Ask Yourself After the Message 237
    Spiritual and Physical Completion Actions 238

SECTION VII: The Last Chapter 241

Chapter 36: God Bless You 243

    Notes 247
    Selected Bibliography 251
    About the Author 255
    Note to the Reader 257
    Prayer for a Personal Relationship With the Lord 259

ACKNOWLEDGMENTS

I give sincere and profound thanks to:

> Jack Cody, my high school speech and debate teacher, who opened the door to public speaking for me.
>
> My parents, Jim and Maravene Barnett, who allowed me to miss Saturday workdays at home so I could compete in speech and debate tournaments. Special thanks to my mother, who always encouraged my speaking endeavors and showed me how to write my first speech.
>
> Pastor Henry Wright and Pastor Anita Hill, who introduced me to belief in the Word.
>
> Pastors Kenneth W. and Lynette Hagin and the teachers at Rhema Bible Training College, who poured their hearts, minds, and years of dedicated service to God into their teaching. I especially thank Kenneth E. Hagin, Tony Cooke, Bill Bush, David Beebe, Doug Jones, Jim Andrews, Marvin Yoder, and Billy Joe Watts. Thank you to Billy Joe Watts for the subtitle of this book; he taught about preaching with "power, passion, and purpose."
>
> Frank Hultgren and the teachers of the Ministry Training and Development Institute at Oral Roberts University.[1]
>
> Billy Joe Daugherty of Victory Christian Center in Tulsa, who made time to talk with me about preaching. For eight years, I watched him preach effective, Scriptural messages that met people's needs, touched their hearts, and helped them deepen their relationship with God.
>
> Dr. Cal Easterling of Oral Roberts University, who encouraged me and gave me valuable feedback in the early manuscript stages.
>
> Sue Rhodes Dodd, who critiqued the first manuscript with wisdom and skill. She helped me become a better writer.
>
> Cecilie Croissant and Amani Fam, who critiqued the manuscript from a theological perspective. Their comments helped fine-tune this book.
>
> Rena Fish for her superb editing, and Angie Zachary for her excellent proofreading.
>
> All my friends who read the manuscript and offered suggestions.

INTRODUCTION

So, as much as in me is, I am ready to preach the gospel to you that are at Rome also. For I am not ashamed of the gospel of Christ: for it is the power of God unto salvation to every one that believeth; to the Jew first, and also to the Greek. (Romans 1:15–16)

What makes an interesting, dynamic, and highly effective preacher or speaker? Is that description only for the small percentage of people who are "natural-born" speakers? Or can those qualities be taught? Here is good news: many of the skills and qualities of naturally gifted speakers can be taught. Even if public speaking is not an area of talent for you, you can become an interesting, dynamic, and effective speaker if you embrace the tools taught in this book.

Speaking for God: How to Preach and Speak with Power, Passion, and Purpose offers specialized public-speaking and ministry training to build, prepare, and equip preachers, student preachers, and Christian speakers. *Speaking for God* is not a scholarly theological book. It is a practical handbook that you can use even if you do not have a college degree, Bible-school training, or seminary background.

Scriptural preachers, teachers, pastors, and evangelists are all speakers for God. Lay people who speak in public about the goodness of God are also speakers for God. Even though there are differences in their job description and anointing, I have lumped these speakers into one category (speakers for God) and called them preachers or speakers.

I am a Christian communication and public-speaking coach. I have been a seminar leader, member of the National Speakers Association, results coach, teacher, and speech pathologist. I am also a Bible-school graduate and trained as a pastor. Every job I have ever had has depended on my verbal communication skills.

When I was a student in ministerial school watching my peers preach in preaching class, I prayed,

> LORD, *if only I could tell them some of the things I know about public speaking, it would make preaching easier for them. It could reduce their struggle and take years off their learning curves.*

A few days later I helped a fellow student on a preaching assignment. In five hours of coaching, she shifted from fear and discouragement into energetic confidence as she learned to get herself out of the way and lift God up to be glorified through her message.

For months, I mulled over the wealth of public-speaking information that tumbled out of me when I coached. I thought of all the people around the world who have been called to speak God's messages. I realized I knew information about public speaking that could help them, and I discovered that God was nudging me to write this book. He impressed upon me the need for His preachers to be given professional speaking and ministry information that could make them more effective.

No matter what my career titles have been, I have always done three things: teach, coach, and encourage. I pray that this book will teach, coach, and encourage you to step up to a new level and enlarge your territory as an effective speaker for God. I yearn to see God's speakers develop into what He intends them to be. The gospel needs to be preached. The day of salvation is now!

Come and develop the gift God placed within you. Embrace the part of this book that is meant for you. And when the LORD says, "Go—preach the good news," step forward into your calling.

God bless you,
Pam Barnett

Note: This book is for every preacher in the body of Christ. Because of that, I have attempted to quote preachers from a variety of churches and denominations. If I have included a preacher's name in this book, it does not mean that I endorse everything that he or she teaches. It simply means that his or her illustration was helpful for the concept being discussed.

SECTION I

FOUNDATIONAL INFORMATION FOR THE PREACHER

CHAPTER 1

PREACHING BASICS

One afternoon in the fall of 1997, I sat with a pastor and ten other people in a small chapel in the heavily wooded, rolling hills of Georgia. I was sick and heartbroken. Through the window, I watched red and yellow leaves detach from toothpick-like trees and float to the ground. A gentle breeze swayed the branches. Mockingbirds caroled back and forth. The physical setting was one of peace. But instead of peace, I was filled with anguish.

With tenderness, the pastor led us into Isaiah 54. After fifty minutes of preaching, the message suddenly became a conduit for the mercy of God to touch me. The anguish, like a massive chunk of black coal, dropped out of me. I grabbed on to the revelation that I am not rejected. I am accepted in the Beloved. No matter who else loves me or does not love me, God loves me and accepts me in Christ.

What makes magnificent preaching? What causes some preachers to be so effective that God's truth is received and lives are transformed? That is the prayed-for end result of this book.

When I graduated from Bible school, I realized God wanted me to take my public-speaking knowledge, join it with ministry training, and write a book that would make His preachers and speakers more effective. When preachers increase their effectiveness, more souls will come into the kingdom. More Christians will mature in Christ and rise up to the positions God has for them. God's love will reach all nations.

What factors lead to Holy Spirit-led, inspired preaching and speaking? How can you position yourself for the anointing? How can you become the dynamic and persuasive speaker you were meant to be?

Speaking for God will give you tools to develop your potential as a speaker and keys to unlock your gift as a preacher. It will teach you how to preach Scriptural messages that meet people's needs, touch their hearts, and help them deepen their relationship with God.

This book will help you:

- Learn the secrets of riveting speakers and highly effective preachers.
- Move beyond anxiety and fear of public speaking.
- Connect with and relate to your audience.
- Hold the attention and interest of your listeners.
- Write memorable, purpose-driven messages.
- Use imagery to anchor your message in people's hearts and minds.
- Meet the needs of your audience.
- Improve your message delivery.
- Prepare and protect your voice and throat.
- Increase your confidence as a speaker.
- Avoid common mistakes made by preachers and speakers.
- Merge the natural and supernatural aspects of preaching.
- Transfer God's love to people.
- Position yourself for the anointing.
- Preach with purpose and new power.
- Get out of your own way so you can accomplish God's job.

Before we launch into public-speaking training, I want to lay the foundation for this book with basic ministry-development concepts.

When I attended Bible school, I learned not to make assumptions about my fellow students. I discovered they all had different knowledge, opinions, and even different beliefs. I realized I had no idea what others believed or thought unless they told me. Because of that experience, I feel it is important that we first discuss basic information about preaching. So let's start at the beginning and consider some questions.

WHAT IS PREACHING?

First and foremost, preaching is an offering of the heart. It flows from the heart of God into the heart of the born-again preacher and then to the heart of the listener. Let's keep this heart-based foundation in mind as we grab onto a practical, working definition of *preaching*. For the sake of simplicity, we can use Warren and David Wiersbe's definition from their book, *The Elements of Preaching*. "Preaching is the communicating of God's truth by God's servant to meet the needs of people."[1]

WHY DO WE PREACH?

Search your heart. What is your motivation for preaching? Why do you want to preach? Make sure you are not preaching to acquire fame, power, or prestige. A preacher needs to be dedicated to achieving what God wants to achieve and to preach as a yielded vessel. Why do you preach? Here are motivating factors to consider.

We preach because:

- We love and revere God.
- We understand the good news of what God did for humans through Jesus Christ.
- We are convinced that all humans need to know Jesus as Lord and Savior.
- God has *called* us to preach, and we have said yes to the call.
- We feel we *must* fulfill the call of God on our lives.
- The Holy Spirit has put an intense yearning in us to speak God's good news.

We preach to bring the love of God to men, women, and children. We are to be conduits—pipelines—through which the Holy Spirit can flow to minister to people. Preaching is not about us. It is about the greatness of God.

What a blessing it is to be called to bring the message of God's goodness. And what a responsibility! *"How beautiful are the feet of them that preach the gospel of peace, and bring glad tidings of good things!"* (Romans 10:15)

WHAT IS THE GOAL OF PREACHING?

What are you trying to accomplish? What is the purpose of preaching?

Basic Preaching Goal

The basic goal of preaching is the restoration of all humans back into relationship and right standing with God—similar to the position Adam and Eve had before they disobeyed, but better.

Why Do People Need to Be Restored?

When Adam and Eve disobeyed God in the Garden of Eden, God's glory lifted off of them, and they became separated from God because of their sin. Since that event, which is called the fall of man, *"all have sinned, and come short of the glory of God"* (Romans 3:23). No matter how nice or kind a person may be, he or she has sinned. Humans do not have the power to cleanse themselves of sin. Every person needs to be restored because everyone has sinned.

How Does Restoration Take Place?

Restoration and the ability to live in the new reality of being the righteousness of God in Christ are accomplished through salvation, baptism, sanctification, discipleship, edification, and equipping for service.

What Methods Are Used to Achieve Restoration?

Through the power of the Holy Spirit, we preach, teach, minister healing, and cast out evil spirits. We also encourage others, seek to be a good example, love and care about people, and obey God. We follow Jesus' example.

WHAT IS MOST IMPORTANT WHEN YOU PREACH?

Do you need a beautiful voice? Do you need to know more Scripture than anyone else? Do you need to use big theological words to impress people? No, no, and no.

This book emphasizes personal relationship with God (through His Son, Jesus Christ), character development, prayer, preparation, moving beyond fear, connecting and building relationship with the listeners, following the lead of the Holy Spirit, and attaining public-speaking and message-writing skills.

Are speaking and writing skills the most important things? No. Most important is that you submit your heart to God and follow His lead so you can preach the right message, at the right time, to the right group of people, in the right way. Throughout this book, please keep the following statement in mind:

> **Basic Preaching Statement**
>
> When you preach, it is important that you care about the people and meet their needs by delivering a Scriptural message, with sincerity, in your own unique way, as you follow the lead of the Holy Spirit.

WHY SHOULD A PREACHER LEARN PUBLIC-SPEAKING SKILLS?

Some people think that taking time to develop public-speaking skills is not necessary if the preacher is anointed. What they don't acknowledge is that preaching is the working together of a combination of factors in the natural and supernatural realms.

You can be anointed to speak for God, but if you have not learned how to project your voice and speak clearly, you may not be heard. If you have not learned how to use stories, anecdotes, and illustrations, your message may not be understood or remembered. If you have not learned how to create memorable wording, your message may not be influential or inspirational. If you have not learned to speak without voice abuse, you may lose your voice. If you have not learned how to deal with stage fright, you may not detect the leading of the Holy Spirit.

Will public-speaking skills lead you to manipulate the audience? No. They are tools that will help you communicate more effectively. Would you be chosen to ride a bike in an Olympic race if you had never learned to hold the handlebars and balance? Of course not. Just like learning to ride a bike, effective public speaking depends upon the acquisition of certain skills.

Important Facts About Speaking Skills

Public-speaking skills that are used properly will never create a lack of authenticity. They will never get in the way of the message. They create connection with the audience and build confidence in the preacher so he can get himself out of the way and deliver the message with clarity and inspiration.

Public-speaking skills are technical details that can be compared to David's skill in using the slingshot. He was anointed to kill Goliath. But in order to slay Goliath (do God's work), David had to be proficient using a slingshot. He probably developed that skill through years of daily practice.

Public-speaking and writing skills do not create the success of the preacher. They don't take the place of being a willing and obedient servant of God. But they are important foundational building blocks upon which the anointed preacher stands.

CHAPTER 2

PREACHING IS A RELATIONSHIP EVENT

The ability to preach with power, passion, and purpose reflects a deep and abiding love relationship with God. It reflects trust in the Word of God. And it reflects loving concern for the well-being of the listeners. In short, the ability to preach with power, passion, and purpose begins in relationship.

Have you ever heard the expression "You can't see the forest for the trees"? Sometimes when people focus on details, they lose sight of the big picture or overall view. (They study individual trees but fail to notice the forest.)

Because this book is filled with a multitude of details about speaking, it is important we keep in mind some overall concepts regarding preaching. Along with the Basic Preaching Statement and the definition of preaching found in the previous chapter, we can add the following big-picture concept.

PREACHING IS A RELATIONSHIP EVENT

Preaching is not a scientific, competitive, or performance event. It is a relationship event. Relationship reflects connection. Relationship and connection develop through communication. Effective preaching does not occur without effective communication.

Some people who teach classes think all they have to do is speak about a subject in order for learning to take place. That is not true. Communication is not a one-sided event. It involves both a sender and a receiver. When you communicate, verbally or nonverbally, you send a message that will be received accurately, inaccurately, or not at all. If your message is not received accurately, effective communication has not taken place.

Three-Way Relationships

In a relationship, people communicate back and forth. There are three back-and-forth relationships that may be active while you preach.

1. You and God

    God speaks to you; you receive the message. You send a message; God receives it. He responds; you receive. And back and forth it goes. It is a communication two-step dance: message sent and message received.

2. You and the Listeners

    You will send messages; they will receive them or not. They will send messages; you will receive them or not.

3. The Listeners and God

    God will be communicating with every audience member. They may or may not notice His communication. Some of them will be communicating with Him.

A Positive Relationship

In the training of professional speakers, preachers, and teachers, there is an important saying: *People don't care how much you know until they know how much you care.* A person with a wealth of information can talk for hours, but the listeners may be resistant if they don't feel the speaker cares about them. Preaching is a relationship event, and the relationship should be positive.

One of my mother's friends is ninety-nine years old. He is intelligent, active, and kind—and he has been a Christian a long time. When he and I were chatting about this book, he said, "I hope you will tell the preachers how to treat people right." In my experience, quite a few people feel they have been harmed, disrespected, or treated unkindly by pastors and preachers they have known.

Preachers need to care about people and show them they care. How do you let people know you care about them? How can one preacher speak on a Scripture and people feel helped and supported, while another preacher speaks from the same Scripture but the listeners feel scolded and beaten down?

Think about preachers you have heard who conveyed warmth, love, and acceptance. What words made you feel accepted? What tone of voice? What was it about them that caused you to feel they cared about you?

I am not suggesting you copy their behavior or do something phony. I am suggesting you increase your awareness. Love is an action word. Learn to communicate it.

We must care about people, care about communicating the message, and care about representing God correctly. Kenneth W. Hagin of Rhema Bible Training College said, "Never underestimate the importance of a loving heart, loving words, and loving actions."[1]

CHAPTER 3

HOW TO CONNECT WITH THE AUDIENCE

Can you speak with power, passion, and purpose without relating to and connecting with your listeners? We noted in the previous chapter that preaching is a relationship event, and a relationship reflects connection.

I attended a service in which the preacher chatted comfortably with the audience—asking us questions, predicting how we might respond, and sharing stories of her life to demonstrate her points. She seemed to know what our objections would be, and she encouraged us to move beyond them. As I left the meeting, I thought to myself, *This is amazing. I was one of three thousand people, but I feel like I had a personal conversation with the preacher.*

Connecting with your audience lies at the heart of effective preaching. Below you will find many ways you can connect with your listeners.

MEET THE NEEDS OF THE AUDIENCE

The needs of the human race are not new. They are as old as human history. We all have a multitude of needs at any given moment in time. We have physical, mental, emotional, and spiritual needs.

One of the best ways to connect with people is to meet their needs by addressing issues that matter to them. When people attend classes, listen to a speaker, or attend church, they want something that relates to their lives—something that will make a difference—something that will help them. That is why people often ask themselves, *Why should I listen? What's in it for me?*

How can you meet people's needs? Show them how the Bible relates to their lives. Let the Word of God instruct, comfort, correct, and strengthen them.

Examples of People's Needs

- If people are afraid, they need help to trust God and stand in faith.
- If people are grieving, they need comfort.
- If people don't know Jesus as their personal LORD, they need salvation.
- When people face seemingly insurmountable odds, they need to know what God recommends they do.
- When people experience unforgiveness, resentment, bitterness, anger, and retaliatory thoughts, they need help to forgive and to establish new patterns of thought and behavior.
- When people are sick, they need God's healing touch.
- All people need to know what God thinks, what He offers, and what He requires. They need to be taught the Bible.

When Charles Stanley (of In Touch Ministries) preaches on the love of God the Father, he works to meet people's needs by helping them overcome their thought-life obstacles. He verbalizes what people may be thinking, and then he answers their objection. He will say something like this:

> You may say, "God could not possibly love me after what I've done." Well, He does. He loves you very much. You may be thinking, *But Pastor, you don't know what I've done.* I don't know, but God knows. And He still loves you.

People need God's comfort, peace, and wisdom. They need to know how to get along with others, what to do when they're afraid, how to control their anger, how to receive God's love, how to resist temptations, how to deal with discouragement and depression, and how to grow closer to God.

When you meet people's needs with Scriptural truth, you are offering them God's love. What an excellent way to connect.

SHOW THE AUDIENCE YOU CARE ABOUT THEM

Some preachers are adept at conveying warmth and caring. But others seem cold or even harsh when they preach. Some preachers care about people but don't know how to communicate that they care. I know of a pastor who cared about the people in his congregation, but he had a brusque and impatient personality. He was criticized for "not having much heart." The criticisms hurt and frustrated him. He learned to reveal his heart by making caring statements from the pulpit.

The apostle Paul communicated his love and care for people. Throughout his New Testament writings, he seems to be a person who developed loving relationships. In 1 Corinthians 16:23–24 he says, "*The grace of our Lord Jesus Christ be with you. My love be with you all in Christ Jesus. Amen.*" In Philippians 1:2–9 he tells the people that they are in his heart, that he longs for them, prays for them, and thanks God for them.

How Can You Communicate to Your Listeners That You Care About Them?

In our daily relationships, we show people we care by giving them our attention and our time. We make eye contact. We listen and are patient. We convey respect and accept them. We take their problems seriously. We smile with our eyes, not only our mouths. We encourage them, speaking words of concern. We rejoice with them, and we mourn with them.

Tell your listeners your hopes—that you want God's best for them. Let them know you understand their challenges, have compassion for them, and do not condemn them. Speak to their hearts as well as their heads.

Examples of Caring Statements a Preacher Might Make

- God has a good plan for your life! I want you to discover that plan and walk in it.

- I want you to be well and healthy. I want you to get your life back.
- We love and appreciate you. We want to see you prosper. We want you to triumph over the difficulties that have pulled you down.
- I pray for you every day. I love you, and God loves you.
- Why am I preaching about this? Because I care about you. I want God's blessings to be poured out upon you and your family.
- God bless you!

Mention Your Sacrifice and Commitment to God

Most people don't know what you go through to be able to speak for God. They don't know about the Bible study, prayer, fasting, and sacrifices you make in order to hear from God on their behalf. Occasionally, you might share a comment about your preparation process.

I have heard preachers say something like this: "Some people think I just stand up here and God fills my mouth with the right words. I wish it were that easy. I've been praying all week about today's message. But Saturday came, and I still did not know what God wanted me to say. My family went boating on the lake without me. I stayed behind and fasted and prayed so I could receive God's message for you.

"I want you to know I take my calling to preach very seriously. I have a commitment to God that I will seek His guidance for every message. He knew ahead of time you would be in this meeting. And He knows what you need. I don't. Not until He tells me. I thank God that He told me. Did I sacrifice? Yes. Was it worth it? Yes. I want you to receive every good thing God has for you."

Pray for Them

We believe in the power of prayer. We believe in the compassion and mercy of God. We believe He answers prayer. Pray for your listeners out loud in the service.

Paul, on behalf of the people he cared about, recorded the magnificent, Holy Spirit-written prayers found in Ephesians 1 and 3, Colossians 1, and 1 Thessalonians 5:23. He sent the prayers in his letters to them so they would know what he was praying.

At the end of the service, when you pray over your listeners, your prayer can touch their hearts and comfort them. Don't miss this opportunity to bless them and demonstrate that you care.

SHARE SOMETHING OF YOURSELF WITH THE AUDIENCE

Personal Anecdotes

Share something about yourself that relates to your message. Personal anecdotes that demonstrate one of your points are an excellent way to do this. When you share a personal story, you invite the listeners into your life as friends. They feel they know something special about you. It connects them to you and is fun for them.

Joyce Meyer, a best-selling author and traveling minister, is an excellent example of a preacher who uses personal anecdotes to make her points. Many people identify with her and learn from her because her life is a testimony of how God can lift us up out of horrible troubles and transform us.

Sometimes audience members look at a preacher and think, *Oh, he has it all together. Life is easy for him. He hasn't had the troubles I have had.* Their thinking causes them to feel disconnected and distant from the preacher.

You have not had a specific audience member's troubles, but you have had your own. Because you are human, you have had challenges, hurts, and fear. You can connect with and encourage your listeners when you share a struggle, a mistake you made, or a frightening situation—and how God helped you rise above it. You can inspire your listeners and create connection when you teach by personal example.

Note: Don't share a personal struggle unless you already have victory over it.

Note: Ask the Lord if it is all right to tell a specific personal story. He knows how the divulging of that information will affect you in the future.

Find a Common Point of Connection

Share something of yourself that relates to the audience. Traditional public-speaking training says to find something you have in common with your listeners and mention it. Was your grandmother born in their town? Did you vacation there once? Have you eaten the maple syrup they produce?

Speak From Your Heart

If you preach a message that matters to you, you preach from your heart and offer the message to the hearts of your listeners. Tell them why you care about it. Be genuine and sincere.

SHARE SOMETHING YOU HAVE NOTICED ABOUT THEM

Another way to connect is to *mention something about their situation*—something that matters to them. Do they have a professional sports team? Is their city known for lovely architecture? Did a horrible disaster recently occur in their town?

You could also *mention to them something about themselves*. The apostle Paul used this technique when he spoke in Athens. He noticed that the Athenians had an altar dedicated "To The Unknown God," whom they worshipped. He used this information to connect with them.

"Then Paul stood in the midst of Mars' hill, and said, Ye men of Athens, I perceive that in all things ye are too superstitious. For as I passed by, and beheld your devotions, I found an altar with this inscription, TO THE UNKNOWN GOD. Whom therefore ye ignorantly worship, him declare I unto you" (Acts 17:22–23).

Billy Graham is a classic example of someone who established rapport by mentioning something about his listeners. He might comment on their sports teams, famous people from their town, current news events that affected them, main industries, etc. Sometimes he arranged for a famous local person to come up and testify. If a tragedy had occurred recently, he talked about it and then segued into his evangelistic message. He often said something like this:

> The recent earthquake brought fear, devastation, and death. None of us knows how long we will live. We don't know when our last day will be. But sooner or later, we will all die. When that happens, only one thing is important…

When you watch preachers speak, notice what they do to create connection and rapport.

AUDIENCE INVOLVEMENT TECHNIQUES

Good teachers involve their students. When you teach God's Word, involve your listeners. Appropriate audience involvement techniques increase attention, understanding, and retention. They also facilitate connection and relationship between you and the listeners.

In this section, we are shifting to specific public-speaking techniques. I am sure you will recognize these communication tools. Most of the highly effective preachers and public speakers use at least some of them.

Greet the Audience

The first speaker on the program (the announcer, worship leader, etc.) will usually greet the audience and make some kind of welcoming comment. A simple greeting by the first speaker is a relationship-building statement. It conveys a message of *Hi. I see you, I care about you, and I welcome you. I am glad you came.*

When several speakers are scheduled, sometimes it is not advisable for succeeding speakers to also say good morning and chitchat. It can slow the momentum of the meeting and weaken your opening. Watch other preachers. Notice which ones give a greeting before they preach. Notice the effect it has on you and what order they are in the speaking lineup. Some preachers always do a greeting. Others rarely do one; they simply launch into a story or opening statement. For every preaching situation, you will need to decide whether a greeting will build relationship or reduce the impact of your opening.

Be Conversational and Make Eye Contact

Speak in a conversational manner, not in a formal preacher's voice. Look at people. Speak directly to them. If you cannot see their faces, look at where you think their eyes are.

Ask Questions

When you ask the audience a question, it engages them in the thinking process. It keeps them involved. Instead of just making statements, every now and then ask a question. The listeners may or may not respond out loud. But they will have thought about it. After you ask the question, pause. Give them time to think.

A preacher could open with: "How many of you have ever seen the movie *The Sound of Music*?" He then would develop his theme around the opening question. The question may be more spiritually direct and to the point. The preacher may ask:

- "Do you know that God is for you and not against you?"
- "Have you ever been angry at God?"
- "Do you wonder where God was in the midst of the recent hurricane tragedy?"

D. James Kennedy, pastor of Coral Ridge Presbyterian Church in Fort Lauderdale, Florida, gave us this example of using questions: "Can you save yourself with self-help programs or good works? The Bible says, 'No!' Why is that? And why is Jesus Christ the only way to heaven?"

When you ask a question, you can:

- Ask for a show of hands in response to the question.

    "How many of you _____?"

- Ask for a verbal response.

    Have them say, "Yes," "No," "Amen," or "Hallelujah" in response to a question (i.e., "Have you found John 3:16 in your Bible? If you have, say hallelujah.")

Caution: Regarding Using the Word Amen as if It Were a Question

- Some preachers are insecure and keep saying "Amen?" They nervously wonder if the listeners agree with them, so they seek a sign of approval. Train yourself not to do this.

- Other preachers make a negative statement, then say "Amen?" For instance, "Sometimes things go wrong. You can't pay your bills; your kids drop out of school; your spouse wants a divorce. Amen?" A common definition for *amen* is "So be it." Don't ask your listeners to say "so be it" regarding a negative situation.

Questions to Be Answered Silently

Some questions are meant to be answered silently in each listener's brain. A preacher might say, "Proverbs 28:1 says, *'the righteous are bold as a lion.'* You are the righteousness of God in Christ. Are you bold as a lion? Do you want to be? In what situations does God want you to be bold?"

You might ask:

- "What would you do if _____?"

    Example: "If you are focusing on God's ways, *what would you do if* your restaurant bill were less than what you really owed?"

- "Has this ever happened to you?"

    Example: *"Has this ever happened to you?* You start to tell someone about Jesus, but you stop because you think they might not like you anymore."

Rhetorical Questions

Rhetorical questions are not meant to be answered out loud. Usually, we assume every listener knows the answer to the rhetorical question.

Examples:

1. *"Can two walk together, except they be agreed?"* (Amos 3:3)
2. *"Is my hand shortened at all, that it cannot redeem? or have I no power to deliver?"* (Isaiah 50:2)
3. "Do our children deserve our time?"
4. "Is it important to develop patience?"

No harm is done if a listener answers the question aloud, as long as the speaker does not make the person feel stupid. I saw a church announcer reply to someone who had answered his rhetorical question. The announcer said, "That was a rhetorical question; you were not supposed to answer it." Maybe he thought he was making a joke, but his words sounded like a rebuke.

The more involved an audience becomes, the more likelihood that some members will answer aloud. This is good. It means they were actively listening. Sometimes when people answer a rhetorical question, it is fun for them. And it anchors the answer in them with an increased strength.

In churches where the preaching style is interactive, listeners may respond verbally. Be ready for them to answer or not. Don't let their reply or lack of one throw you off balance.

Sentence Fill-In

When you are talking about a well-known subject, you can use the sentence fill-in technique. Every now and then pause and let the listeners fill in a key word in the sentence. Use Scriptures that are well known.

Examples:

1. *"Bless the LORD, O my soul, and forget not all his _____"* (Psalm 103:2).
2. *"God resists the _____, but gives grace to the humble"* (James 4:6). Then you can reverse the fill-in: *"God resists the proud, but gives grace to the _____."*

Repeat After Me

You can use the repeat-after-me activity in many ways. Have your listeners repeat your summary sentence, a prayer, or a main point. Have them repeat a faith confession or lead them in repentance.

Examples:

1. "Everybody repeat after me: 'I am the righteousness of God in Christ. I have God's Spirit on the inside of me. I am a new creation because I have accepted Jesus as my Lord and Savior.'"

2. "Everybody say: 'I am the redeemed of the Lord!'"

3. "Let's come to God, repent, and get cleaned up. Just repeat after me: 'Father God, I repent of my doubt and unbelief. I ask You to forgive me in the name of Jesus. I turn away from doubt. I am not a doubter. I am a believer. I believe Your Word, and I thank You for it. And now, just like it says in 1 John 1:9, I thank You for forgiving me and cleansing me.'"

Never underestimate the power of this technique. It puts the listeners into the position of doers. They step into an active role instead of a passive one. It can break the power of negative forces in the spiritual realm and help people move forward. I have seen God honor the use of this ministry method again and again.

Note: Speak slowly, use short phrases, and pause when you lead listeners in a repeat-after-me sequence.

Read Scripture Together

Ask the people to read Scripture out loud with you. Wait while they locate the verse in their Bibles. Read slowly and clearly so they can keep up with you.

Misread Scripture

When the listeners are reading along in their Bibles with you, you can read the Scripture incorrectly. Then wait for them to catch it. For example, when reading Mark 9:23 aloud: *("Jesus said unto him, If thou canst believe, all things are possible to him that believeth"),* you can change the word "all" to "some." So you say, *"Jesus said unto him, If thou canst believe,* some *things are possible to him that believeth."* If no one catches the error, ask them, "Is that what it says? Let's look at this again." Someone will correct you. Then you can say, "Oh, *all* things. How many things?"

Say to Your Neighbor

You can tell the listeners to say something to people who are sitting near them.

Examples:

1. "Greet your neighbor and tell them you're glad they came."

2. "Say to your neighbor, 'You're in the right place.'"

Stand Up and...

Preachers get to move around during a service. Sometimes the listeners have been sitting a long time. They may need to change positions. You can tell them to stand up and do something.

Examples:

1. "Let's all stand up and sing to the LORD."

2. "Would you please stand for the reading of the Word?"

3. "Let's everybody stand up. Say hello to three people before you sit down."

You May Be Thinking...
You May Say to Yourself...
You May Be Wondering...

You have probably heard preachers use this technique. It is one way to address objections, clear up confusion, or let the listeners know you understand them. It also helps create the feeling of a conversation. Choose one of these three introductory phrases, and then insert what you think the listeners are thinking or feeling.

Examples:

- "You may be thinking, *I'm all alone. I have no one to depend on but me.*"
- "You may say to yourself, 'If I had more time or energy, I'd do it.'"
- "You may be wondering, *Why did God let this happen? Doesn't He care about me?*"

Corporate Amen

When you pray a prayer aloud on behalf of the group, you can end by saying, "And all the people said _____." (You pause and let them say "Amen" with you.) This may seem too insignificant to mention, but it is not. When the people say "Amen," it identifies the prayer as their personal prayer, and it becomes a corporate prayer. It involves and unifies the group.

MORE WAYS TO CONNECT WITH AND RELATE TO THE AUDIENCE

Along with meeting the audience members' needs, caring about and respecting them, telling them you care, praying for them, sharing something of yourself with them, and involving them in your message, what else fosters a positive relationship? What causes the listeners to feel connected to you?

It helps if you are trustworthy and kind (not sarcastic or bitter). It is also important to be a person of integrity and godly character so your listeners will want to be connected to you.

As you present the message, you can watch the listeners' reactions and adapt or comment when appropriate, move around on the stage to get closer to the audience, and smile at appropriate times.

If you don't connect with your listeners, you might as well be talking to the walls at home. The tools in this chapter will help you connect. Because preaching is a relationship event, connection is vitally important.

CHAPTER 4

HOW TO BUILD CREDIBILITY AS A PREACHER

Have you ever heard the children's story *The Boy Who Cried Wolf*? The boy in the story thinks it is fun to yell, "Help! Help! Wolf! Wolf!" so that the townspeople will run to save him. When they arrive with their weapons, there is no wolf attacking the boy. The boy does this over and over. Eventually, the townspeople stop running to help him when he cries, "Wolf!" Then one day, a wolf really does attack the boy. He yells, "Help! Wolf!" but no one comes.

The boy had destroyed his credibility with dishonesty. His history of lying kept the townspeople from perceiving the truth of his final call for help.

In order to help people, you have to be credible and believable. What you say has to be reliable. People need to *feel* they can trust you. You need to be sincere and honest, and they must *see* that you are.

WHAT IS A CREDIBILITY GAP?

If people doubt your truthfulness, honesty, or integrity, if they don't believe what you say, or if they feel they cannot trust you or your interpretation of Scripture, you have a credibility gap.

HOW PEOPLE DETERMINE YOUR CREDIBILITY

It is the listener who decides whether you are credible or not. It is not enough that you are truthful. You must be truthful and also *be perceived* as being truthful.

People will decide about your credibility based upon the following:

1. How likable you are.
2. The information they have about you—regardless of whether it is true or not.
3. The truthfulness of your words.
4. Their *perception* of the truthfulness of your words.
5. The accuracy of your Bible interpretation.
6. Your values—as demonstrated by your words and behavior.
7. Your history of service as a minister.
8. Your character traits.
9. Whether your beliefs match their beliefs.
10. Your appearance.
11. Your ability to communicate effectively with sincerity.

You don't have control over another person's evaluation of you, but there are things you can do to develop your credibility.

HOW TO DEVELOP CREDIBILITY

Many factors influence a person's evaluation of you, but first of all you need to live a life of integrity, stay away from pride, and help people trust you.

LIVE A LIFE OF INTEGRITY

But in a great house there are not only vessels of gold and of silver, but also of wood and of earth; and some to honour, and some to dishonour. If a man therefore purge himself from these, he shall **be a vessel unto honour, sanctified, and meet for the master's use, and prepared unto every good work**. (2 Timothy 2:20–21)

Character traits are important to God and to people. We often choose from whom we will learn based upon what we know about them.

You Are the Message

As a speaker for God, you are not just delivering a message. You are the message. The Bible tells us the teacher will be held to a higher standard than others. I know people who have rejected Christianity because of the behavior of Christians they knew. When a minister behaves in wrong ways, people may become disillusioned and step away from Christ.

I have been in services where the personality problems or skewed perception of the preacher is what I learned about. The message did not teach me. The preacher's behavior did. As a public speaker, I often remind myself of the "you are the message" reality, lest my audience members say, "Who you are and what you do speak so loudly I cannot hear what you are saying."

In a preretirement interview, after serving Mt. Zion Baptist Church in Tulsa, Oklahoma, for fifty years as pastor, Dr. G. Calvin McCutchen, Sr., said, "It's more than just preaching the gospel. You've got to be the gospel as well."[1]

Be diligent in seeking God and His ways for your character development. You should regularly check your integrity levels.

What Is Integrity?

A person with integrity is honest, trustworthy, and dependable. One definition of *integrity* is "the condition when a person's actions and words match their values, which are based upon godly principles."

If you say you will do something, can you be counted on to do it? When you make a mistake, do you admit it, or do you give excuses (reasons)? If you misjudge your timing and are late, do you pretend there was a traffic jam? Do you tell people you will pray for them, but you don't? Do you claim to be friends with famous ministers when actually you only met them once? Do you make up stories for your messages and pretend they are true—or pretend that some other person's experience happened to you?

Do a self-evaluation and ask yourself, *When I speak, am I being honest? Is what I am saying really true?* The majority of preachers don't lie outright, but some are dishonest in other ways. They exaggerate. I have seen ministers stretch the truth about the number of healings that occurred at their meetings. I now doubt the truth of all their other statements.

In his book *How to Prepare Sermons*, William Evans comments, "The preacher must also be truthful. Exaggeration is lying, stretching the truth is lying, and a lie in the pulpit is worse than a lie anywhere else."[2]

Here is an interesting detail about integrity problems: the person with the problem may not know about it.

One Friday afternoon, I walked behind two pastors on the way to a seminar. Pastor #1 said to Pastor #2, "Do you have your message for Sunday yet?"

Pastor #2 laughed and replied, "No, but I'm going to get up there and say, 'I had a dandy message prepared for you today, but I believe the Holy Spirit wants us to go in a different direction. So we're going to follow His lead and find out where He takes us.'"

I was stunned that he would lie to his people and, without qualms, reveal it to a fellow pastor. Apparently, he did not realize he was lying and that it was wrong.

We may need the help of other people in detecting our integrity problems and character flaws. It's good to have honest friends and family members who will confront us and hold us accountable.

STAY AWAY FROM PRIDE

> *A bishop then must be blameless, the husband of one wife, vigilant, sober, of good behaviour, given to hospitality, apt to teach;... Not a novice, lest being lifted up with **pride** he fall into the condemnation of the devil.* (1 Timothy 3:2, 6)

Visible pride can damage your credibility. When I observe pride in a preacher, I am not as open to receiving his or her teaching. When I was in training as a minister, I asked my mentor what I needed to guard against. She replied, "Pride. The way to stop it before it gets started is to immediately give God the glory anytime someone gets healed or helped through your ministry."

Give Glory to God

In a church service I attended, the speaker announced that one of their pastors had coordinated a successful community prayer program along with other local churches. The congregation began to clap and cheer because *their* pastor had spearheaded it. The pastor realized the error, and as she walked toward the lectern, she redirected the group by saying, "Let's all praise Jesus! It's His work—let's give Him all the glory! Thank you, Jesus!"

If you watch the healing evangelists, you will notice they often say something like, "Jesus is the One who healed you! It wasn't me! Jesus is the healer!"

When your message helps people, some of them will thank you. Think about how you will respond.

HELP PEOPLE TRUST YOU

The establishment of trust is a crucial issue for preachers. You must have people's confidence before you can help them. How can you earn their trust? It helps to do the following: Be kind and caring. Have integrity; be dependable and accountable. Be organized, confident, and humble. Dress appropriately. Keep confidentialities. Exhibit confidence in the Word of God and obedience to it. Be a good role model. Work to stay emotionally well-balanced, be consistent, and avoid moral failure.

Avoid Moral Failure

You can probably think of some famous preacher who lost a respected position because he or she yielded to temptation. Temptation often comes in the form of greed, pride, or sexual immorality. Watch out for greed in your relationship to money. Watch out for becoming puffed up and thinking you are more important than you are. Watch out for sexual temptations.

You have a responsibility to keep yourself, your motives, and your actions pure. As a minister, you may encounter individuals who are sexually attracted to you. Don't flatter yourself into thinking this is happening because you are so special. They don't really want you. They want to be attached to the power that comes from the anointing and the office you hold.

Be aware of what you would secretly love to hear someone say to you. "Oh, you're so handsome, wise, gifted, smart, anointed, etc." If you are not aware of it, you will be an easy target for deception to seduce you. The moral failure of a preacher harms the work of God and causes people to distrust preachers.

Model Obedience to the Word of God

Effective preaching may include examples of your struggle to become obedient to the Word of God. Your testimonies of how God helped you move away from difficulties like bitterness, sickness, drugs, immorality, lying, or fear can increase people's trust in you. As you share your journey of God working in you, the listeners can realize you experience the same challenges they do. But you demonstrate the fact there is victory in Jesus. There is not only deliverance, but joy, hope, and peace when living in obedience to God.

Be a Good Role Model

Do your best to live what you preach. The apostle Paul mentioned several times the importance of being a good role model. *"Those things, which ye have both learned, and received, and heard, and seen in me, do: and the God of peace shall be with you"* (Philippians 4:9).

One Sunday when I was a new Christian, I went out to lunch with a pastor, his family, and some church members. The pastor had reserved a section of the restaurant for us, but when we got there, only half of the section had been saved. The pastor spoke to the waitress in charge. Angry words flashed back and forth. Both of them were frustrated and upset. I thought to myself, *This is interesting. I wonder what will happen next.*

After this confrontation, all of us except the pastor went to get our food from the buffet. As we sat down and began to eat, I watched the pastor. He did not get his food. He sat totally still, with head bowed, hands folded in his lap, and eyes closed. He stayed that way for about ten minutes. Then he called the waitress over to the table. He said loudly enough for all of us to hear, "I want to apologize for the way I spoke to you. I was wrong. I should not have gotten angry or spoken crossly. I'm sorry. Will you forgive me?"

Her shoulders relaxed, the look in her eyes softened, and she replied, "Yes, I should not have spoken that way either."

The pastor added, "I want you to have a good day. I don't ever want to be the cause of someone having a bad day."

As a new Christian, I was watching to see how a professed man of God handled the frustrations of everyday life. Just as I watched him, people watch you to see if you practice what you preach. Your behavior in daily life can affect your credibility in the pulpit.

MORE WAYS TO BUILD CREDIBILITY

1. Develop your public-speaking skills and your confidence.

2. Preach as often as you can to develop a track record.

3. Go on mission trips. They will give you your own true miracle stories to tell.

4. Gather testimonials from people your preaching has helped. If appropriate, tell these stories to demonstrate how God has used your ministry. Share the testimonials without breaking confidentiality guidelines. When the listeners hear these true-life stories, it will build their faith and help them benefit from your message.

5. Demonstrate your knowledge. Speak about something you have earned the right to talk about through experience or study.

6. Write your own introduction, and give it to your introducer. Include in it some of your accomplishments that relate to your position as a preacher. This has nothing to do with pride. The goal is to give the listeners information that will prepare them to receive your message.

7. Demonstrate your concern for people.

Also, show your enthusiasm for living as a child of God. Let the joy of the LORD be a part of your lifestyle. When people see happy and compassionate Christian ministers, Christianity becomes attractive and believable.

CHAPTER 5

GUIDELINES FOR A GUEST SPEAKER OR TRAVELING MINISTER

I saw a traveling minister preach and then say to the senior pastor, "Let's pray a prayer of agreement. Will you agree with me in prayer?" The guest speaker then prayed an unscriptural prayer. The senior pastor was in an uncomfortable position. Should he let it go, or should he embarrass the guest preacher by saying, "That is not scriptural, so I cannot agree with you." What did he do? (It was not a big doctrinal issue.) He let it go.

Traveling ministers need to be alert and aware. There are pitfalls to avoid if you are a guest speaker in a church.

The Pastor Is the Spiritual Authority for His Own Church

The local pastor has been set in position by God. When you are a guest speaker in a church, you are under the pastor's authority. Don't do or say anything that would be objectionable to him.

Discuss possible topics with the pastor. Stay within the guidelines he gives you. If you have theological disagreements with him, don't try to correct his theology when you speak in his church.

As a general rule, a visiting speaker should not correct the congregation. Correction is the pastor's job. If you think the Holy Spirit has given you a message of correction, discuss it with the pastor. He is responsible for the teaching of his people. If you bruise or confuse them, he must help them recover. Don't create extra work for him.

The stepladder of spiritual authority is important to God. He cares about His line of order. Defer to the pastor; he is in charge. Give honor to whom honor is due.

Counseling Audience Members

In his book *The Traveling Minister's Handbook*, Marvin Yoder states, "Refuse to counsel members of the congregation, unless the pastor requests that you do so."[1] If the pastor asks you and you agree to privately counsel an audience member, don't do it alone. The pastor or another representative of the church should be with you. Ministering in partners can help protect you from claims of misconduct or misunderstandings regarding what you said or did.

The Altar Call

If the pastor wants you to give the altar call, ask him how he does it. Find out if the church has an altar prayer-ministry team to assist you.

Ministering to the Pastor and His Family

You may be in a position to minister to the pastor and/or his family. Get ready. Fill yourself with the Word of God and ground yourself in peace. Keep confidentiality unless the law requires you to report a situation. Being a spiritual leader can be a lonely experience. God may have sent you to speak at a church so you could minister to the pastor's family.

Watch Out for Bitterness

If the church takes up an offering for you but they never give it to you, don't get bitter. I heard a traveling minister say that when churches neglected to send him the offering they had promised, he prayed for them and sent *them* an offering just to bless them. He said his prayer and offering erased any inclination he had toward resentment and kept him in a position to minister for God.

Keep a Balanced Perspective

Don't be impressed if people say you are a better preacher than their pastor. If you had to do all the work of a local pastor *and* come up with two or three new messages a week, after awhile you probably would not look so spectacular to them. Not only that, but a traveling minister has a different anointing than a pastor.

When you are in balance, you work together to do God's work—in humility—knowing that the power behind your effectiveness comes from God.

CHAPTER 6

THE ANOINTING

The Spirit of the L*ord* *is upon me, because he hath* **anointed** *me to preach the gospel to the poor; he hath sent me to heal the brokenhearted, to preach deliverance to the captives, and recovering of sight to the blind, to set at liberty them that are bruised, To preach the acceptable year of the* L*ord.* (Luke 4:18–19)

The first time I spoke for God and delivered a scriptural message was in a chapel service. The audience was a group of sick people. They were unusually attentive. All eyes were riveted on me as I spoke. No one moved or made noise. After the message, one of the long-time Christians said to me, "Pam, you have an anointing to speak."

I was not familiar with the term "anointing," but I knew from my public-speaking background that God had given me special ability in the area of speaking. I was used to people paying attention, but this audience's reaction was beyond what I had expected. Why were they so attentive? What made the difference? The anointing of God was present.

WHAT IS THE ANOINTING?

Some ministers talk a lot about the anointing. Others never mention it. But whether they mention it or not, the anointing is necessary if a minister is to succeed in God's work.

First I want to mention that every Christian has an anointing. Christians have been chosen and set apart by God and have received the Holy Spirit who indwells them. Using the word *anointing*, 1 John 2:27 indicates that every Christian has an "endowment of the Holy Spirit." (See *The New Strong's Exhaustive Concordance of the Bible*, Greek word #5545.)[1]

Our discussion of the anointing and how it pertains to preaching will focus on two other aspects of the anointing.

1. The anointing is a setting apart for service. Individuals are chosen by God for specific types of work.

2. The anointing is also the presence and power of God. It is God's power, God's ability, and God's enablement given to us to do His work. The anointing is an empowering for service. It is the Holy Spirit in action, making our work productive.

Without the anointing, you only have your own skills to rely on. That is not enough. They are totally inadequate to do the work of God. But through the supernatural power of the anointing, God can use your abilities and skills to accomplish His purposes.

ANOINTED FOR A CERTAIN OFFICE

The first aspect to consider is the anointing of a person to fill a particular office or position. The person is chosen to function in a certain type of job. For instance, a person is anointed to be an apostle, prophet, pastor, evangelist, teacher, or helper.

Aaron and his sons were anointed as priests to minister to the LORD. Moses anointed them with oil to appoint, consecrate, dedicate, purify, and sanctify them for their service as priests. *"And he poured of the anointing oil upon Aaron's head, and anointed him, to sanctify him"* (Leviticus 8:12). The job of priest was not by personal choice. God set them apart and chose them to function in the office of priest.

In 1 Samuel 10, we see Saul being anointed with oil (set apart) to be the king of Israel. In 1 Samuel 16, Samuel anoints David with oil to be the next king over Israel.

Vine's Complete Expository Dictionary of Old and New Testament Words makes the following statement regarding "to anoint" in the Old Testament:

The Old Testament most commonly uses *māsah* to indicate "anointing" in the sense of a special setting apart for an office or function. Thus Elisha was anointed to be a prophet (1 Kings 19:16). More typically, kings were "anointed" for their office (1 Samuel 16:12; 1 Kings 1:39).[2]

Ministry of Helps

Some people are called to the ministry of helps. They work faithfully in the background. They answer phones, set up chairs, cook meals, etc. They do whatever is needed.

Years ago I did not realize that God calls people into these positions, and they enjoy their work. My neighbor is called to the ministry of helps. She loves being helpful. Once when she found out I needed a ride to the airport, she said, "May I take you to the airport? I would love to drive you there." When she made that offer, all of a sudden I gained insight into God's calling to the ministry of helps. Some people have an anointing for it.

What Has God Called You to Do?

In Romans 1:1, Paul says, *"Paul, a servant of Jesus Christ, **called** to be an apostle, **separated** unto the gospel of God."*

You have been set apart by God to function in a certain type of job. What is it? Did He call you to be a preacher? Or does He want you to be a greeter, usher, or something else? What gifts has God placed in you? What do you yearn to do? What interests you? Answering questions like these will help you discover your calling.

Donald E. Demaray, in his book *Introduction to Homiletics*, comments:

> When God initiates the call, a sense of inner urgency results. John Henry Jowett, in that classic, *The Preacher: His Life and Work*, says an authentic call is no mere preference among alternatives. "Ultimately, the called person has no alternative: all other possibilities become dumb: there is only one clear call sounding forth as the imperative summons of the eternal God."[3]

Be sure of your calling. If you are going to preach, it is important you know God wants you to do it. Speaking for God as a preacher has special challenges no other job has. If you know God has called you to preach, that knowledge will help you hold steady when times get tough.

THE SITUATIONAL ANOINTING: THE INTENSIFIED POWER AND PRESENCE OF GOD

I call this second aspect of the anointing the *situational anointing*. It is that extra intensification of God's presence, bringing His power in unusual strength into a situation or person. It is usually a momentary experience, not a long-term event.

I once attended a church service led by an Argentine pastor. Halfway through the message, he asked us, "Can you understand my English?" When we all nodded yes, he said, "When I'm under the anointing, the Holy Spirit tells me more English words than I normally know."

After the meeting, I went up to him and began talking. He looked at me politely with a smile on his face. I soon realized he did not know the English words I was using and that it was true—while preaching under the anointing, he used more English than he actually knew in regular life.

When you preach and the anointing is present, God will be working in the hearts, minds, and bodies of the listeners. He may heal people's bodies or their broken hearts. He may give them comfort, guidance, or a deeper revelation of His love for them. He may convict people of sin and show them the need to repent. He may deliver them from fear, shame, grief, pornography, alcohol, or any other oppression.

The Holy Spirit may put the situational anointing upon you and give you boldness in witnessing, or He may heal a person when you lay hands on them and pray. He may give you a superior memory and excellent flow of words as you preach.

Through the anointing, the Holy Spirit brings His presence, ability, and power into situations in an infinite variety of ways.

THE ANOINTING IS NOT LIMITED TO ANY DENOMINATION OR PREACHING STYLE

Different ministers have different preaching styles. Some preachers are calm, intellectual, and matter-of-fact. Others are more enthusiastic, dynamic, and inspirational. Some are emotional. Some are not. Some are loud. Some are soft.

When the anointing intensifies upon a preacher, it is not unusual for him or her to speak louder and become bolder or more dramatic. But a quiet, soft-spoken preacher can be just as anointed and effective. No matter what your preaching style or denomination, if you are doing what God told you to do at the moment that He wants you to do it, you are a candidate for the anointing.

JESUS NEEDED THE ANOINTING AND SO DO WE

In Luke 4:18, Jesus said, *"The Spirit of the L*ORD *is upon me, because* ***he hath anointed me to preach the gospel....***"

Acts 10:38: *"How* ***God anointed Jesus of Nazareth*** *with the Holy Ghost and with power: who went about doing good, and healing all that were oppressed of the devil; for God was with him."*

Even though Jesus was God incarnate, He was a human being. Not only was He the Son of God, but He was also the Son of Man. As a human on this earth, He had to be anointed by God, just as you have to be anointed by God in order to do His work.

The word *anointed*, in Acts 10:38, is number 5548 in the Greek part of *The New Strong's Exhaustive Concordance of the Bible*. The word that was translated as *anointed* has the following explanation: "...chrio, *khree'-o*; prob. akin to 5530 through the idea of *contact*; to *smear* or *rub* with oil, i.e. (by impl.) to *consecrate* to an office or religious service:–anoint."[4]

According to *Vine's Complete Expository Dictionary of Old and New Testament Words*, the usage of the word *chrio* is confined to "sacred and symbolical anointings."[5]

Jesus was set apart and empowered to do God's work. He transferred His authority to us (His followers) and commanded us to go preach the gospel (Mark 16:15–20). He said we would do greater works than He had done (John

14:12). Obviously, we cannot do greater works in our own strength. Jesus needed the anointing, and so do we.

WHAT BLOCKS THE ANOINTING?

We depend on God's anointing to empower us to do what He calls us to do. We pray, fast, study, meditate on Scripture, and seek God's face and His ways. Yet sometimes it seems the anointing eludes us. Why? Sometimes it is not present because we are blocking it.

I have known individuals who did not know why the LORD did not move them into Christian leadership. One particular person regularly criticized the church leaders. Another one often voiced opinions contrary to the Word of God. Sometimes people don't perceive the ways in which they block the anointing.

Distraction

Anything that distracts us can block the anointing. We need to take care of the details of daily life, but if we want the anointing God has for us, we will carve out time for God and learn to keep our focus on Him.

We need to say no to things that intrude on our God-focus. For instance, I don't answer the phone or the door if I am praying. I don't allow low-priority details to intrude on high-priority activities.

What is likely to distract you? Are any of these distractions typical in your life?

- Being mentally scattered or disorganized
- Staying too busy or being overwhelmed with responsibilities
- Not putting God in first-priority position (i.e., paying more attention to your hobby than to God)
- Being distracted by circumstances (i.e., meetings, job loss, illness, other people's problems)
- Being distracted by emotions (i.e., happiness, sadness, anger, fear)
- Being distracted by entertainment or fun
- Being distracted by the past

If preachers answer questions or minister to individuals right before they preach, the anointing for preaching may be diminished. When I attended a small church, I noticed that if people told the pastor their problems right before he preached, he would be unfocused and scattered in his opening statements. Some churches have staff members whose job is to intercept anyone who tries to talk to the preacher before he preaches.

Charles Spurgeon, the famous Baptist preacher of the 1800s, made this comment:

> You know what one cold-hearted man can do, if he gets at you on Sunday morning with a lump of ice, and freezes you with the information that Mrs. Smith and all her family are offended, and their pew is vacant. You did not want to know of that lady's protest just before entering the pulpit.[6]

The distraction can be a tiny event. I attended a series of meetings led by two pastors. On the first night, one of them mentioned that distraction is the enemy of the anointing. The second night, one sat next to me while the other one preached. My attention was on the preacher until I thought I might start coughing. I tried to quietly unwrap a cough drop, but the paper wrapping made a magnified crinkling sound.

The pastor next to me looked at me and then worked to screen out the distraction. He moved forward in his seat, rested his forearms on his knees, and leaned intently toward the podium, trying to keep his focus on the preacher.

My noisemaking—followed by his reaction—anchored in me the learning of the moment. Distraction is the enemy of the anointing.

Sin

Sin includes not only ten-commandment-type sins, but also other ones like speaking against God's anointed, being proud, or fearful.

The writer of Hebrews encourages us: "*... let us lay aside every weight, and the sin which doth so easily beset us, and let us run with patience the race that is set before us, Looking unto Jesus the author and finisher of our faith*" (Hebrews 12:1–2a).

Any sin you have not repented of (confessed and turned away from) can block the anointing God has for you. In his book *From Faith to Faith*, Kenneth Copeland comments, "But sin hinders the Spirit's flow. And only as we rid ourselves of it will the power and glory of God be manifested through us."[7]

According to 1 John 1:9, *"If we confess our sins, he is faithful and just to forgive us our sins, and to cleanse us from all unrighteousness."* It is important that we stay cleaned up and sin-free through the process God has provided.

Not Pursuing God Diligently

You can block the anointing by being lackadaisical. An inadequate prayer life, inadequate worship, and inadequate time in the Word can all block the anointing. Marvin Yoder, in his book *The Traveling Minister's Handbook*, comments,

> A minister who does not have a devotion time on a regular basis can get by for a while. If he continues with no devotions, soon he will lose that fresh touch in his message; he'll have no reserve left when a crisis comes along; and eventually, when he goes to minister to someone, the power of God will be nowhere to be found.[8]

Misunderstanding What God Wants You to Do

Sometimes we do work that God did not ask us to do. Some people have had unpleasant experiences pastoring. Perhaps God did not place them in their positions. If God did not call you into the office you are trying to fill, you may end up frustrated and defeated. There is no substitute for being in a God-chosen job, at a God-chosen time, in a God-chosen place.

POSITIONING OURSELVES FOR THE ANOINTING

As preachers, we desire to be in the center of God's will, hearing His voice and flowing in the anointing. We are well aware that we are not the power behind the words we speak.

Without the supernatural power and ability of God to bring about His desired results in our listeners, we become simply public speakers, orators, or someone who can "turn a good phrase." Becoming clever public speakers is not our goal.

Where does the anointing come from? It comes from God. Obviously we know that, but it is important for us to remember this fact. The anointing is put on people according to God's will, not according to our own will. We cannot order it, control it, or demand it. We cannot produce it or force it to come upon us.

God decides when and upon whom to put the anointing, yet there are conditions that will set the stage for it. When we meet those conditions, we position ourselves for anointed ministry.

Develop Your Relationship With God

Your relationship with God is the foundation of your call to preach. Make it top priority. Give it your time, energy, and commitment. As you establish deeper intimacy with the Lord, you will learn what grieves Him and what quenches the Spirit. You will become sensitive to Him and to His leading.

In the year 2002, Dr. Frank Hultgren was the director of the *Ministry Training and Development Institute* at Oral Roberts University.[9] He was also the chaplain to the professors. When he taught our class on the laying on of hands and prophecy, he mentioned that the previous week he had prayed for, laid hands on, and had an individual, prophetic word for each of five hundred students at a meeting. To have a personal, prophetic word for five hundred people, one right after another, is an unusual manifestation of the anointing.

When I asked him about the anointing, he said:

> Many people think I spend a lot of time praying. I don't. I spend a lot of time basking in the presence of the Lord, fellowshipping with Him, praising him, worshipping Him, loving Him. Being in His presence is worth more to me than watching television, sleeping, or eating. People can get confused in their efforts to serve God. Here's the important thing: just love Him. Spend time loving Him and receiving His love.

God does not anoint us because we are well-educated, smart, or clever. He does not anoint us because we are eloquent speakers or have lovely voices. He does not anoint us because we look professional or have a stately bearing. God is looking for hearts that love Him, are submitted to Him, and are in sweet communion with Him.

Develop Positive Character Traits

You may have a calling, but is your character developed adequately to sustain it? Here in the United States, every now and then a preacher falls into disgrace from immoral or illegal conduct. It becomes a high-profile, public event. At other times, a preacher's problem remains more private and is embedded in criticalness, self-centered ambition, impatience, etc. Some preachers don't have the character development to handle the fame or power that may come as a result of their position.

The LORD wants you to mature in His ways. If you resist the temptations coming your way and develop godly character, it will help position you for the anointing.

Be Willing and Obedient

> *If ye be willing and obedient, ye shall eat the good of the land.*
> (Isaiah 1:19)

I have had personal experience with the anointing and disobedience. I remember a time when the LORD's presence was strong upon me. I knew I was supposed to go home and write messages. In my spirit were the words, *I must be about my Father's work! I must be about my Father's work!* It was a pressing, urgent, passionate statement. I was so excited! God had answered my prayers and vaulted me to a new level. But as I drove toward home from the meeting I had just left, I saw the mall with all of its stores. I thought to myself, *I've been immersed in the things of God for the last eight days. I could use a relaxation break— maybe just two hours. That will leave me plenty of time to write messages.*

What happened? I went shopping. When I got home, the glorious presence of God had lifted off of me. I sat down to write a message, but I was on my own. Nothing came to me.

The LORD seems to put an anointing on a person and then watches to see how the person responds. I had passed smaller tests, but this bigger one, I failed.

I am glad the calling of God is without repentance. (He doesn't change His mind.) In the years since that event, He has led me step by step—growing me up in Christ and refining me for service. I am grateful that He works with us and helps us turn our mistakes around.

Some preachers don't socialize or do hobbies on Saturday. Instead, they pray and spend time with God because they know they need the anointing when they preach on Sunday.

For a preacher, "the good of the land" includes the anointing. There is a price to pay for it. It is obedience. We must surrender our own desires and agendas and be willing and obedient to His.

Be Flexible and Yield to the Spirit's Leading

You are a co-worker with God. You are God's partner, and partners work together. To flow in the anointing, you must learn to yield to the Holy Spirit. Be willing to lay your message aside if the Lord indicates you should go in another direction.

Sometimes preachers interrupt their message to prophesy or speak a word of knowledge from the Lord. The preacher, all of a sudden, might say something like, "Someone is being healed at the base of your spine right now. You were in a car accident, and God is healing you." In order to yield, they have to be flexible, attentive, and ready.

There Is a NOW Timing to the Situational Anointing

The Holy Spirit may impress upon you the need to pray for a specific group of people during the service. That might mean the anointing is present to help them right then. If you understand there is a NOW time for the anointing, you can move forward obediently and do the Lord's bidding. But if you think you can put aside the Lord's direction until a more convenient moment, the anointing may lift and leave.

The Lord may have you change the order of the service or eliminate part of it. You might be partway through the message when, all of a sudden, you know it is time to do a call for salvation. Now. Not twenty minutes from now. Preachers often conduct the salvation call at the end, but I have seen Holy Spirit-led preachers give the salvation call in the middle or even at the beginning of the service (contrary to their regular pattern).

I was on vacation and about to climb into a kayak when a woman I had just met told me she had skin cancer. Immediately, without any thought on my part, the words, "I rebuke that skin cancer!" came up out of my spirit and tried to be spoken. But I closed my mouth to stop them. I did not want to be rude and interrupt the woman. If I had been attentive to the Holy Spirit, had not had my brain in vacation mode, and had not been afraid of offending her, God could have worked a miracle for her through me.

If we miss the timing for the situational anointing, the opportunity is gone.

Always Keep in Mind How Wonderful God Is

Frank Hultgren made this comment: "When we have a deep appreciation of who God is, we minister out of reverential knowledge. And our ability to minister is greatly increased because it comes out of awe, and gratitude, and humility, and reverence, and yieldedness. And God loves it!"[10]

Anointed preaching flows out of our love relationship with God. It flows out of our obedience to Him. It flows out of our ability to hear His voice and follow it. It flows out of our willingness to lay down our own agendas. It flows out of our faith in the Word and our trust in God. Anointed preaching flows out of a lifestyle of submission to Him.

> ... *Not by might, nor by power, but by my spirit, saith the* LORD *of hosts.* (Zechariah 4:6)

CHAPTER 7

WHAT IS THE GOSPEL?

For God so loved the world, that he gave his only begotten Son, that whosoever believeth in him should not perish, but have everlasting life. (John 3:16)

When I was a child, my family attended a Christian church. My mother taught Sunday school, and my father served on the finance committee. We went to all the church functions, but there was a problem. I never heard the gospel preached.

I heard sermons on good works and morals (thou shalt not smoke, drink, or swear). I never heard the word *sin* and did not know there was a hell.

One Sunday I attended both church services so I could listen intently for information about a wonderful God. None was offered. When I graduated from high school, I left the church—thinking I knew what Christianity had to offer. I remember deciding, *Well, God is not here in the church. I might as well go see what the world has to offer.*

Several times in my adult life, Christians witnessed to me about Jesus. But their words made no sense. They would ask, "Have you accepted Jesus Christ as your Lord and Savior?" What did that mean? Why would I need a savior? Or they might say, "Are you saved?" What did I need to be saved from?

One time I asked one of them, "Why would I need a savior? I'm doing fine; my life is good." The man paused as if stunned by the question. He finally replied, "Your sin. You are a sinner." I was a sinner? I was not aware of having any sin. I was one of the nicest people I knew.

One Christian who witnessed to me was a critical and unkind person. I thought to myself, *If she thinks she's going to heaven and I'm not, then she is crazy. God knows I am a nicer person than she is.* I thought good deeds, good behavior, and a kind heart were how God would choose people for heaven.

I decided Christians were strange people and it was best to avoid them. I would crack a joke to myself saying, "The only thing I need to be saved from is them!"

Once I attended a church service in which the pastor did not tell us about Jesus, but he ended by quoting Revelation 12:11, *"And they overcame him by the blood of the Lamb, and by the word of their testimony; and they loved not their lives unto the death."* Then he said, "So this week, testify to someone about what Jesus has done for you."

I thought to myself, *Well, what has Jesus done for me? I don't know that He has done anything for me.*

I had spent hundreds of hours in Christian churches and never heard the gospel. I had no idea why God sent Jesus to earth. I had no knowledge of what Jesus had accomplished. And I did not know that I was not in right relationship with God. Why was the salvation gospel not preached?

One of several reasons may have accounted for this.

1. The preachers did not know the gospel message, or
2. They did not know how to communicate it, or
3. They did not realize they were not preaching it, or
4. They thought the Holy Spirit was supposed to do all the work, so they did not need to teach on salvation.

Romans 10:13-14 clearly tells us that a preacher needs to preach about Jesus so people can believe and get saved. *"For whosoever shall call upon the name of the Lord shall be saved. How then shall they call on him in whom they have not believed? And how shall they believe in him of whom they have not heard? And how shall they hear without a preacher?"*

The most fundamental information a preacher needs to have is the knowledge of the salvation gospel and how to communicate it. Then he needs to make a commitment to preach it over and over again.

WHAT IS THE GOSPEL?

In a broad sense, the gospel is the good news of God's Kingdom and His provision of salvation through His Son, Jesus. Using that definition, we can say the gospel begins in Genesis 1:1 and ends at Revelation 22:21.

But more typically, when we speak about the gospel, we are referring to a narrower focus, highlighting the good news of the salvation God provides for humans through the substitutionary death, burial, and resurrection of His Son, Jesus. Part of salvation is the forgiveness of sin and deliverance from the eternal penalty of sin (you won't go to hell when you die). Salvation provides God's gift of eternal life with Him.

Gospel Summary

God is our Creator, and He loves everyone. He made a way for people to end up in heaven even though we have all sinned. His Son, Jesus, came to earth in the flesh. Jesus was born of a virgin. Because He did not have an earthly father, He did not inherit the sin problem that all other humans are born with. (When Adam disobeyed God in the garden of Eden, sin came upon the human race.) Jesus was without sin and lived a sinless life. He died on a cross to pay the penalty for the sins of all people. He rose from the dead. He offered His shed blood as the payment for our sins so we could be forgiven and cleansed if we choose Him as Lord and Savior. If we reject Jesus, we will have to go to hell to pay for our sins when we die. Jesus is alive forevermore. He is seated at the right hand of God the Father. Jesus said, *"Ye must be born again"* (John 3:7). *Born again* means born from above.

You become born again when you:

1. Repent of your sins and ask to be forgiven (Acts 20:21).

2. Believe in your heart that Jesus is the Son of God who died on a cross to pay for your sins and rose from the dead (Romans 10:9).

3. Believe and speak that Jesus is LORD and that you accept Him as your personal LORD and Savior (Romans 10:9–10). (You give your heart and your life to Father God by accepting His Son, Jesus.)

This is also called "getting saved." When you become born again (get saved):

- You are forgiven of your sins (Colossians 1:14, Ephesians 1:7).
- You become a new creation (2 Corinthians 5:17).
- You become a child of God (John 1:12, Galatians 3:26).
- You are cleansed of sin and become the righteousness of God (2 Corinthians 5:21).
- The Holy Spirit comes and lives in you (John 14:17, 1 John 4:4, Galatians 4:6).
- You are delivered from the power of darkness and translated into the kingdom of God's dear Son (Colossians 1:13).
- You receive life everlasting. You will end up in heaven, not hell (John 3:16).
- You are accepted in the Beloved. You are now "in Christ" (Ephesians 1:6).

Salvation is amazingly wonderful, and it's a free gift! Ephesians 2:8 says, *"By grace are ye saved through faith; and that not of yourselves; it is the gift of God."*

ANNOUNCING THE GOOD NEWS OF SALVATION THROUGH JESUS CHRIST

When you speak the gospel message about salvation through Jesus Christ, some people will accept Jesus as their LORD and Savior if you tell them a simple statement like this:

> God loves you. He sent His Son, Jesus, to die on a cross to pay the penalty for your sins. Jesus rose from the dead. If you believe

this truth and ask Him to forgive you of your sins, be your Lord, and save you, He will. Would you like to do that now?

For people who don't know they have sinned, you can start with the topic of sin and say:

God loves you, but there's a problem. The Bible says we have all sinned (Romans 3:10, 23), and the penalty for sin is death (Romans 5:12, 6:23). Sin separates us from God. But the good news is that God sent His son, Jesus, to die on a cross to pay the penalty for our sins (John 3:16, Romans 5:8). You can be forgiven of your sins and not have to suffer for them in hell if you call on Jesus to save you and be your Lord. He will give you everlasting life (Acts 2:21, Romans 10:9–10, 13). Would you like to ask Him to save you now?

Note: You may need to show them from the Bible that they are sinners and have broken God's holy laws. If they don't know they have sinned, they won't see the need for forgiveness or a Savior.

These short gospel versions will help some people, but others may need a more comprehensive presentation. There are four basic areas to cover. Some of the following comments are adapted from:

- Bill Bright's booklet, *Have You Heard of the Four Spiritual Laws?*[1]
- Billy Joe Daugherty's brochures at Victory Christian Center[2]
- LaDonna C. Osborn's book, *God's Big Picture*[3]

I have written this four-point gospel message as if you are speaking it directly to someone. First is a short version, and a longer version follows.

FOUR-POINT GOSPEL MESSAGE (SHORT VERSION)

1. God loves you and has a good plan for your life (John 3:16). But there's a problem.

2. Sin separates people from God. The Bible says all people have sinned, and the penalty for sin is death (Romans 3:23, 6:23a). It also says there is no forgiveness of sins without the shedding of blood (Hebrews 9:22).

3. The good news is that Jesus died for your sins (Romans 6:23).

4. If you ask Jesus to be your LORD and Savior, His shed blood will pay for your sin (Romans 10: 9, 10, 13). You will be forgiven and cleansed. You will become a child of God in right standing with Him. Jesus will give you His righteousness (2 Corinthians 5:21). You won't have to go to hell to pay for your sin. You will receive a reborn spirit and life everlasting.

FOUR-POINT GOSPEL MESSAGE (LONG VERSION)

1. God's Creation

God created everything: the sun, moon, stars, animals, oceans, fish, birds, trees, and flowers. God also created humans. He created people different from the animals. He created people in His own image and likeness. The Bible tells us this in Genesis 1.

> *And God said, Let us make man in our image, after our likeness: and let them have dominion over the fish of the sea, and over the fowl of the air, and over the cattle, and over all the earth, and over every creeping thing that creepeth upon the earth.* ^{27} *So God created man in His own image, in the image of God created He him; male and female created He them.* ^{31} *And God saw every thing that He had made, and, behold, it was very good. And the evening and the morning were the sixth day.* (Genesis 1:26–27, 31)

God created Adam and Eve, the first humans, in His own image and put them in a wonderful garden where all their needs were supplied. They had direct relationship with God, and God loved them.

Note: In some countries, different people groups believe they were descended from alligators or other animals. LaDonna C. Osborn says it is important to explain that all humans were created by God in His image. This knowledge gives people dignity.[4]

God created you. He loves you, and He has a good plan for your life. What keeps God's good plan for you from happening? There is a problem:

2. Satan's Deception

Sin separates people from God.

In Genesis 2:15–17, before God created Eve, God gives Adam the command for staying pure and righteous.

> *And the Lord God took the man, and put him into the garden of Eden to dress it and to keep it. And the Lord God commanded the man, saying, Of every tree of the garden thou mayest freely eat: But of the tree of the knowledge of good and evil, thou shalt not eat of it: for in the day that thou eatest thereof thou shalt surely die.*

After God created Eve, Satan (who is also called the devil) tempted Eve to doubt God. She believed Satan's lies. Because of that, Adam and Eve disobeyed God's order not to eat from the tree of the knowledge of good and evil. When they ate the fruit of that tree, they lost their purity, sin came into them, and a curse came upon the earth. Their sin (their disobedience) brought disease, violence, and death into the earth. Satan received Adam's dominion over the earth and became the god of this world (Genesis 3).

The problem now is that all humans have sinned, and sin keeps us from being in right relationship with God. Romans 5:12 tells us, *"Wherefore, as by one man [Adam] sin entered into the world, and death by sin; and so death passed upon all men, for that all have sinned."*

Romans 3:10, 23 point out that all people are sinners. *"As it is written, There is none righteous, no, not one: ... For all have sinned, and come short of the glory of God."*

In Romans 6:23, the Bible says that we all deserve death because we have all sinned. It says, *"For the wages of sin is death."* God is loving and kind. He loves everyone. But He is also a God of justice, which means that sin has to be punished.

How can we get rid of our sin? How can we escape punishment for it? People try to get close to God by morality, philosophy, or religion. Many people think God will favor them and let them into heaven for being good, honest, nice people, or for giving to the poor, or for praying a lot. God likes it when we pray to Him and do good deeds, but doing good actions does not get rid of sin. The consequence of our sin is spiritual separation from God for all eternity, which means going to hell when we die.

How can we avoid going to hell to suffer for our sins?

Here is the good news:

3. Christ's Substitution

Jesus died for your sins.

The Bible says there is no forgiveness of sins without the shedding of blood. Hebrews 9:22 says, *"And almost all things are by the law purged with blood; and without shedding of blood is no remission."* (Remission means forgiveness.)

God loves us so much! He does not want us to have to pay the penalty for our own sin. So He sent His Son, Jesus, to earth to be crucified on a cross to pay the price for the sins of all humans. Jesus suffered for your sins so you can be forgiven and cleansed.

Jesus died in our place; He took our place on the cross. He was our substitute. Romans 5:8–9 says, *"But God commendeth his love toward us, in that, while we were yet sinners, Christ died for us. Much more then, being now justified by his blood, we shall be saved from wrath through him."*

If we return to Romans 6:23 and read the rest of it, God shows us His wonderful provision of mercy and salvation. *"For the wages of sin is death; but the gift of God is eternal life through Jesus Christ our Lord."*

God has a wonderful, free gift of salvation and eternal life for you. Do you have to do anything to claim your gift? Yes! Here's the important part:

4. Our Restoration

God wants to forgive you of your sins. But you have to choose Jesus as your Lord and Savior so His shed blood will pay for your sin.

The only way to God is through His Son, Jesus, because no human has the power to get rid of his or her own sin. God's great gift of restoration and redemption is summed up in John 3:16: *"For God so loved the world* [all humans]*, that he gave his only begotten Son, that whosoever believeth in him should not perish, but have everlasting life."*

If we accept Jesus into our hearts as Lord and Savior, His blood washes us clean of our sins, our identity changes, and we become children of God. John 1:12 tells us, *"But as many as received him, to them gave he power to become the sons of God, even to them that believe on his name."*

The important thing to know is that each of us must make a personal decision to accept Jesus as Lord and Savior if we want our hearts to be made right with God. Going to church will not save us from the punishment for our sins. Singing in the choir will not save us. Helping the poor will not save us. Our parents' position as Christians will not save us. We each have to decide for ourselves.

You have to make your own decision. Will you accept Jesus? If you want to be forgiven and cleansed of your sin, receive a reborn spirit and the Holy Spirit of God on the inside of you, and life everlasting—you must accept Jesus Christ as your Lord and Savior.

How do you do that? It's easy to receive God's free gift of salvation! Do these three things:

1. Repent of your sins. (That means confess them, turn away from them, and ask God to forgive you.)
2. Believe in your heart that Jesus, the Son of God, died on a cross for your sins and rose from the dead.
3. Believe and speak that Jesus is Lord and that you accept Him as your personal Lord and Savior.

Romans 10:9–10, 13 says: *"If thou shalt confess with thy mouth the Lord Jesus, and shalt believe in thine heart that God hath raised him from the dead, thou shalt be saved. For with the heart man believeth unto righteousness; and with the mouth confession is made unto salvation… For whosoever shall call upon the name of the LORD shall be saved."*

Wow, that is good news!

Salvation Prayer

If you want to be in right standing with God, be forgiven of your sins, and receive everlasting life, sincerely (from your heart) pray aloud this prayer with me. Just repeat after me.

> Dear Father God, I thank You that You made me and You love me. I believe in my heart that Jesus is the Son of God. I believe He died on a cross, rose from the dead, and paid for my sins with His blood.
>
> I repent of my sins. Jesus, come into my heart and be my LORD and Savior. Please forgive me of my sins and fill me with Your Holy Spirit. I confess that Jesus is LORD, and He is my LORD.
>
> Father, I thank You that I am now cleansed, my spirit is reborn, and I will spend eternity with You. Romans 10:13 says that whoever calls on the name of the LORD shall be saved. LORD, I have called on Your name, so I thank You now for saving me and making me new. In Jesus' name, amen.

Note: When you lead people in a repeat-after-me prayer, speak in short sentences or phrases, and pause, so they can remember and repeat what you have said.

PREACH THE GOSPEL

> *And he said unto them, Go ye into all the world, and preach the gospel to every creature. He that believeth and is baptized shall be saved; but he that believeth not shall be damned. (Mark 16:15–16)*

Don't assume your listeners know about salvation. If it is not in your main message, weave it into your altar calls.

SECTION II

HOW TO OVERCOME FEAR OF PREACHING

INTRODUCTION

As he preached, the beginning preacher paced back and forth like a caged leopard. Every little while, a nervous laugh punctuated his speech. Afterwards, one of his friends said to him, "You were nervous."

In any book on public speaking, fear is a topic of importance. Many people become nervous before they speak in public. Anxiety, worry, and fear regarding public speaking are common experiences.

Whether you present a progress report to a review committee or whether you speak to thousands of people, there is pressure on you to perform in a certain way. The audience, the person who invited you to speak, and you yourself have desires, goals, and expectations about the outcome of your speech. You may experience internal pressure that makes the delivery of your message more difficult.

How can you move beyond that pressure? How can you become a good speaker even if you feel terrified? To win victory over fear, we prepare mentally, physically, and spiritually. We work with our thoughts, we work with our bodies, and we pray.

CHAPTER 8

STAGE FRIGHT

If your future father-in-law asks you a controversial question, your palms may begin to perspire, and your voice may tremble as you answer. If your supervisor calls you in and asks about a mistake you made, your blood pressure may rise and your pulse may speed up. The term "stage fright" refers to the physical manifestations of stress, nervousness, or fear when a person is placed in some kind of performance situation.

There are many physical symptoms of stage fright: increased perspiration, dry mouth, fast pulse, increased blood pressure, shaky hands, wobbly knees, trembling voice, shallow breathing, tense muscles, increased adrenaline, memory problems, stiff and unexpressive face, or trembling jaw or lips.

Here is the good news:

1. Stress is subjective. It is in the mind of the beholder. What is stressful to someone else may not be stressful to you. Your perceptions, attitudes, and beliefs create stress or a lack of it. That means you can work with your mind to reduce your stress.

2. Stage-fright symptoms usually only affect the beginning of the message. They tend to disappear as you speak.

3. If you go ahead and speak even in the presence of intense fear, your fear will diminish and lose its grip on you. As you do what you are called to do, fear will become less and less of a factor in your preaching.

Don't let stage-fright symptoms stop you. Many suggestions in the following chapters can help you.

CHAPTER 9

THE BEFORE-SPEAKING ROUTINE

In the front pew of a small country church, I waited for my sister-in-law's memorial service to begin. My brother had asked me to do the eulogy. I was silently collecting my thoughts and praying—praying that God would anoint me to speak and bring comfort to the gathered people, praying that I could bring some of God's Word to them, and praying that I would not sob while speaking. I didn't mind if tears rolled down my face, but it was important that I stay focused on my task.

As I sat quietly in the pew, to my surprise, my legs, arms, and hands began to tremble. Then I noticed my face felt stiff and unexpressive like a mask. All of a sudden, I realized I had forgotten to do the Before-Speaking Routine. I tried to correct the situation by breathing deeply, but it did not stop the shaking.

The service had not started yet, so I walked quickly out the back door. I did a hurried version of vocal and physical warm-ups. When I re-entered the church four minutes later, all of the distress symptoms were gone. As I delivered the eulogy, God gave me extraordinary ability, and I experienced the joy of serving Him even in sad circumstances.

It is important that you develop a Before-Speaking Routine that you always follow before you speak. This routine will decrease your anxiety, strengthen and safeguard your voice, increase your physical expressiveness, and prevent many mispronunciations and stage-fright symptoms. It will also increase the oxygen flow to your brain, helping you access your best thinking ability and your memory. Do the following routine in the hour before you speak:

PHYSICAL WARM-UPS

If you think you are physically fit and don't need to do physical warm-ups, I hope you will reconsider. I learned the following techniques in acting classes. (Actors know that their main tools of communication are their bodies and voices.) Your body and voice need to be warmed up.

In my thirties, I did stage acting. One Saturday I took a TV commercials acting class. Everything we did was videotaped. I did not do physical warm-ups before class because it was not a performance, and I did not feel tense. When I saw myself on camera, I was shocked to see how stiff and wooden-like I appeared.

At the break, I did my warm-up routine. After my second turn in front of the camera, the instructor said, "That was excellent. How did you vault to such a high level?" I replied, "I did physical warm-ups."

I hope you will learn from my experience. You may not *feel* stiff and unexpressive, but you may *look* stiff. Warm up your muscles.

Our Goals in Warming Up Our Bodies Are to:

- Prevent injury

- Prepare our bodies for action

- Calm ourselves down

- Improve oxygen flow to our brains

- Increase our physical expressiveness

- Improve our coordination

Caution: Be careful. Don't do any exercise that creates pain or is unwise for you to do for some other reason. If my exercises are not a good idea for your body, make up your own.

Basic Physical Goal

Gently stretch all major muscles and move every joint.

Physical Warm-Up Exercises

Do *mild* stretching exercises. Stretch in any way that feels good and is safe. I usually go into a restroom stall and do *slow* stretches.

1. General Stretch: Lift your hands and arms over your head and reach toward the ceiling. Stretch sideways, forward, and backward in any way that feels good to your body.

2. Shoulders: Move your shoulders up, down, backwards, and forwards.

3. Head and neck: Move your head down, up, back, and to each side.

4. Face: Exercise your facial muscles. Open your mouth and eyes as wide as you can. Smile as big as you can. Make funny faces. Yawn a huge yawn to stretch the face and throat muscles.

5. Arms: Do swimming motions with your arms. If you have room, swing your arms in figure eights.

6. Hands and Wrists: Open both hands and stretch the fingers wide, then close both hands into a tight fist. Let the hands relax, then revolve the hands in a circle around the wrist, in one direction and then the other. Let the hands hang limply at your sides; shake your fingers as you would to shake water off them.

7. Sides: Lift one arm over your head and slowly bend to one side. Do the same on the other side. Twist your body to each side as if you are turning to look over your shoulder.

8. Legs: Walk in place, lifting your knees high. Bend forward and allow your hands to hang down toward your toes. Slowly ease into the stretch.

9. Feet and Ankles: Stand up straight with your feet apart. Rise up onto the balls of your feet. Go up and down. Then lift one leg forward with pointed toe and revolve your foot in a circle. Repeat this action with the other leg.

This may seem like a lot, but you can do it in five minutes or less. If you don't want to do the above stretches, you can do tense-and-release with all muscle groups. (You tighten a muscle for a couple of seconds, then release it.) This is not as effective as stretching, but it's better than nothing.

VOCAL WARM-UPS

Athletes do exercises that warm up their muscles to perform to capacity. The *vocal cords* and the *articulators* (tongue, cheeks, lips, soft palate, throat) have muscles that need warming up.

Benefits of Warming Up Your Voice

- Greater vocal variety available
- More variation in pitch available
- Less chance of injuring your voice (hoarseness, sore throat, etc.)
- More variety in volume available
- A reduction in fear symptoms (trembling or high-pitched voice)

Benefits of Warming Up Your Articulators

- Less chance of mispronouncing words
- Increased ability to speak quickly and be understood
- Less tension in your face, which will make you look more confident
- A reduction in fear symptoms (trembling jaw, voice, or lips)

Vocal Warm-Up Exercises

You don't need to do all of the following exercises, but be sure to warm up both the voice and the articulators.

Start out slowly and gently. The loudness level should be soft to average. The pitch should start in your comfortable range and only go up a few notes, then down a few notes in the beginning. After some warming up, you will carefully work your way up to higher notes and down to lower ones.

Try to keep the location of the sound in the mask area of the face; you will feel a vibration in the nose or mouth area. Don't strain your voice while warming up.

Humming (voice warm-up)

Keep your lips together, and hum ("m-m-m-m"). Humming places the vibration of sound in the mask area.

1. Song and Scales (voice): Hum a favorite song. Hum the musical scales using notes that are in an easy pitch range.

2. The Pendulum (voice): Think of a pendulum on a grandfather clock. The pendulum swings up on one side, then down to center, then up on the other side. Hum notes that swing up and then down, up and then down. As your voice warms up, go up to higher notes, then down to lower ones with each "swing of the pendulum."

3. Roller Coaster (voice): A roller coaster goes up, then dips down, over and over again. Make your voice do a roller coaster while humming.

4. Fire Engine (voice): Think of the sound a fire engine makes and do it with the "m" sound.

The Horse Whinny (voice)

When horses whinny, they start at a high pitch, and with a shaky sound, they go down in pitch. With your lips closed, make a shaky, nasal sound while you go down in pitch.

Yawn (voice and articulators)

Yawn with a sigh. If people are around, you can yawn with no sound.

Scales (voice and articulators)

Sing the musical scales (la-la-la) within easy vocal range. Then sing them higher and lower, but reduce your volume so you don't strain your voice.

Continue singing scales, but change "la-la-la" to "ba-ba-ba," then "da-da-da," then "ga-ga-ga." Next, sing "la-ba-da-ga." Our goal is to switch back and forth to consonant sounds that use different articulation movements.

Vowels (voice and articulators: cheeks and lips)

Use exaggerated facial movements while you say the long vowel sounds ("a" as in ate, "e" as in eat, "i" as in ice, "o" as in open, "oo" as in pool).

Alphabet Consonants With Long Vowel Sounds (voice and articulators)

Use the consonants in the alphabet in sequence as you say the long vowel sounds. Example:

(b) buh-bay, buh-bee, buh-bie, buh-boe, buh-boo

(c) cuh-bay, cuh-bee, cuh-bie, cuh-boe, cuh-boo

(d) duh-bay, duh-bee, duh-bie, duh-boe, duh-boo

(f) fuh-bay, fuh-bee, fuh-bie, fuh-boe, fuh-boo

Bay, bee, bie, boe, and *boo* is in all the examples. The only change is a different consonant matched with the sound "uh."

Read Out Loud (voice and articulators)

Read your Bible (or any book) quietly out loud. Use distinct and exaggerated pronunciation.

Red Leather, Yellow Leather (voice and articulators)

I learned this exercise from a voice-over artist who worked in Hollywood, California, as the voice of cartoon characters. This exercise is the last one to do in your warm-up series.

Say "red leather, yellow leather" over and over again. Say it quickly. This is a simple exercise but very difficult. At first try, I found it almost impossible to do. But as I practiced, I learned a trick. While you say "red leather, yellow leather," ask yourself silently, "What color?" That will make you emphasize the words "red" and "yellow." You will then find you can do this exercise without biting your tongue or slowing down to a snail's pace.

The ability to do this exercise is a good indication that your articulators are warmed up and ready to serve you well as a speaker.

Simpler Vocal Warm-Up Routine

If you don't want to do so many vocal warm-ups, at least do the following:

1. Yawn.
2. Hum a tune that goes up and down.
3. Read your Bible (or any book) quietly out loud to yourself with distinct and exaggerated pronunciation.

ABDOMINAL BREATHING

Abdominal breathing is a basic tool for any speaker. It will:

- Relax you before a speech
- Calm you down during a speech
- Help your body stop shaking
- Help your voice stop quivering
- Deliver more oxygen to your brain
- Give you more vocal power

Learn how to do abdominal breathing. When you inhale, pull the air all the way down into your stomach area. Your stomach will expand like a balloon. As you exhale, the "balloon" deflates. While practicing, put your hand on your stomach and feel it going in and out as you breathe.

Practice. Take two deep breaths in the midst of different kinds of activities. For example, breathe deeply while you socialize. Don't let it be noticeable. Don't let your shoulders lift up or your chest puff out.

Large arm movements at chest level or higher—where the arms move out to the side—will increase your deep breathing ability. In private, you can do figure eights in large, sweeping arm movements at shoulder level. Or pretend you are an orchestra conductor, arms held high, moving your arms in and out, up and down.

Do two minutes of abdominal breathing in your Before-Speaking Routine.

Note: If you don't practice breathing deeply, you might get dizzy if you breathe deeply during your message.

BATHROOM BREAK

It might be a long time from the beginning of the service until you preach. Some speakers have wished they had gone to the bathroom beforehand. Each of us is different. You know what your body needs. Plan accordingly.

APPEARANCE CHECK

People might not tell you if something is wrong with your appearance. Look in a mirror before you step up to speak. Check your clothing, hair, teeth, nose, and front and back view.

CHAPTER 10

FEAR-REDUCTION TECHNIQUES

When I think of preachers I have seen who exhibited fear reactions, these three examples come to mind:

1. The preacher's hands shook, her voice trembled, and she struggled to hold back tears.

2. The speaker spoke indistinctly in a soft voice, shuffled his feet, and stared at the floor.

3. The preacher kept his gaze riveted on his notes. He spoke hesitantly with long pauses between words. When he ventured to look up at us, he resembled a panic-stricken deer caught in the headlights of a car, and he lost his train of thought.

Is there help for speakers like these? Yes, of course. All competent and effective speakers did not start out as naturals who took to public speaking like a duck to water. They learned from experience and often from training classes and books like this one. And whether they know it or not, most of them use fear-reduction techniques.

I have used the following techniques in many situations. If you use the ones that are right for you, you will be able to vault beyond fear and focus on the task at hand.

FEAR-REDUCTION TECHNIQUE #1
PRAY AND DEDICATE YOUR MESSAGE TO GOD

The Holy Spirit knows who will be in your meeting and what they need. Diligently seek God's guidance. Bathe the message and yourself with prayer. Ask God to help you speak what He wants you to speak—and in the way He wants it spoken.

Proverbs 16:3 says, *"Commit thy works unto the Lord, and thy thoughts shall be established."* Offer your message to God as an act of worship. When we honor God with our work, He strengthens and steadies us.

FEAR-REDUCTION TECHNIQUE #2
KNOW YOUR MESSAGE

Other than praying, if I had to choose one fear-reduction technique, this would be it. Be prepared. If you know your message, have rehearsed it adequately *out loud*, and are passionate about it, stage-fright symptoms will not be as intense.

FEAR-REDUCTION TECHNIQUE #3
WARM UP YOUR BODY AND VOICE

The next most important fear-reduction technique is the Before-Speaking Routine. Physical and vocal warm-up exercises, which were described in the previous chapter, can reduce and even prevent fear symptoms. They are valuable beyond description.

FEAR-REDUCTION TECHNIQUE #4
LEARN BASIC INFORMATION ON
FEAR OF PUBLIC SPEAKING

If you know the following information, it can reduce your nervousness.

1. Fear of public speaking is a common experience.

2. Most of the audience members want you to succeed.

3. Don't expect to get rid of all your nervousness.

4. Nervousness can be used as energy for a dynamic presentation.
5. Anxiety and fear can be greatly reduced and even eliminated.
6. Fear can be a spiritual attack. See Fear-Reduction Technique #15 (*Use Spiritual Weapons*).
7. Fear will increase if you dwell on the thoughts that are creating it.
8. Right before the speech, nervousness will increase if you talk about how nervous you are.
9. Anyone with the ability to carry on a normal conversation can learn to speak adequately in public.
10. Physical exercise can decrease nervousness and fear.

FEAR-REDUCTION TECHNIQUE #5
IDENTIFY YOUR FEARS

You can reduce fear by identifying and dealing with it. Sometimes we don't deal with fear because we don't recognize it. We call it names like "stress, tension, nerves, jitters." When you identify the fear, you may find that it is exaggerated, unrealistic, and probably will not happen. Or the fear may be a reasonable concern that requires preventative planning. The following exercise can help you calm down.

Identify Your Fears

What are you afraid of? Make a list. Write down all your fears. For each fear, fill out a Fear-Buster Chart:

1. Write one fear at the top of a piece of paper.
2. Write down the likelihood of what you fear actually happening.
3. Write down Scriptures that will strengthen you against that fear.
4. Make decisions that deal with the issue.

Example of a filled-out Fear-Buster Chart:

FEAR-BUSTER CHART
Fear: Fear of being criticized   **Likelihood:** This might happen.
Rebuttal Scriptures   1. "The Lord is on my side; I will not fear: what can man do unto me? It is better to trust in the Lord than to put confidence in man" (Psalm 118:6, 8).   2. "Be not afraid of their faces: for I am with thee to deliver thee, saith the Lord. Then the Lord put forth His hand, and touched my mouth. And the Lord said unto me, Behold, I have put my words in thy mouth" (Jeremiah 1:8-9).
Decisions   1. I am going to run the race I was called to run. I am not willing to be intimidated by fear. I am acceptable to God, and my job is to please Him. I refuse to cooperate with a "fear of man."   2. I will preach what God tells me to preach even if people criticize me.   3. If I am criticized, I will listen, consider what is said, take it to God, learn what is valid, and toss out the rest.   4. I will look for the smiling faces in the audience.   5. I will not assume that frowning faces represent criticism.   6. I will stand in the strength of God's love and will not get offended if I am criticized.

If you find that your fear is well-grounded because you are not prepared, do what you can to correct the situation. Then go to God and ask for mercy and grace. Do your best next time to be prepared.

FEAR-REDUCTION TECHNIQUE #6
MONITOR YOUR SELF-TALK

What are you saying to yourself? What thoughts are going through your mind? If you wonder why you feel anxious, tune in to your inner dialogue. Usually a thought comes first, then an emotion.

Sometimes our thought patterns are habits from our past, and we are not aware of them. These are typical limiting statements some people hear as they grow up:

- You're a loser. You're dumb. You'll never amount to anything.

- You're not good enough. You aren't smart enough. You mess up everything you do.

- Keep your mouth shut. You don't have anything important to say.

If you want to gain control over negative emotions, listen to your internal dialogue. Are you thinking, *I can't do this! They'll find out I have nothing to say. I'm going to throw up when I get up there to speak! I'll probably mess this up.*

If you catch yourself thinking negative thoughts, decide to stop. Then take action. Replace negative self-talk with positive, faith-filled statements. Use Scripture.

For example: "The idea that I cannot do this is a lie. I refuse to believe a lie. I refuse to be deceived. I am a preacher. I am grateful to be called to preach. It is written, '*I can do all things through Christ who strengthens me.*' I am going to deliver God's message, and it will bless people. My God is with me. He empowers me. I can do this in His strength, and I will."

If you change to positive self-talk, you will become a happier person, your fears will diminish, and you will set yourself up for more success as a preacher.

FEAR-REDUCTION TECHNIQUE #7
CHOOSE YOUR ATTITUDES

God gives us the opportunity to choose our beliefs and attitudes. We choose how to view and interpret the events of our lives. We can look at our opinions and decide to keep them or not.

Our comments reveal our attitude choices. Here are statements spoken by my fellow students in Bible school before they preached in class:

Negative Comments

- Nobody wants to listen to me. They'll probably pick apart what I have to say.
- I'm afraid they'll find out how little I know. I bet they'll laugh at me.
- I bet they'll be bored when I speak. They'll probably be glad when I sit down.

Positive Comments

- Wow, I can't wait to preach!
- I'm relieved this is God's job. If I were on my own, I'd be scared.
- God is going to help someone through my message.

Suggestions for Creating Positive Attitudes

Decide you have something to offer—something that can help people. Create positive thought statements. Example: "People can benefit from listening to me. I belong up here. God has given me a word for these people."

Beware of black-and-white thinking. Black-and-white thinking is an either/or thought pattern that goes to extremes. It creates a distorted perception (i.e., "The success of my career hangs on the outcome of this message.") Make yourself do balanced, accurate thinking.

Remember you are a co-laborer with God. If God has called you to preach, He will honor your obedience, willingness, and hard work. He will help you preach.

Rejoice in your call to preach. If you have said yes to the call, be happy about it. Expect God to move through you and bless your listeners. Your expectations will affect the outcome. You might as well admit, "I was born to preach. I am a preacher. Preaching is fun. This is what I want to do."

Support other preachers. In Bible school, one of my fellow students said to me, "I missed hearing you preach. I bet you really showed me up." Her words stunned me. We are co-workers. One person plants the seed of the Word, another waters, and God reaps the harvest. Preaching is not a competition. We are all on the same team.

In his book *The Anointing: Yesterday, Today, Tomorrow*, R. T. Kendall says, "I fear that the anointing many of us desire is largely delayed because of a rival spirit. We look over our shoulders and, consciously or unconsciously, compete with one another."[1]

Our attitude choices make life pleasant or unpleasant. And they make preaching a pleasure or an ordeal.

FEAR-REDUCTION TECHNIQUE #8
GET UP TO SHARE

Some people are frightened by the idea of getting up to "preach" or "give a speech." If that is you, then change your idea of what you are going up there to do. Don't go up to preach or give a speech. Instead, go up to share something important to you—with someone who is important to you.

FEAR-REDUCTION TECHNIQUE #9
IDENTIFY HOW YOUR MESSAGE WILL HELP PEOPLE

How will your message help your listeners? If they embrace it and use it, how could their lives change and be better? Concentrate on the audience and how the message will help them.

FEAR-REDUCTION TECHNIQUE #10
LET GO OF PERFECTIONISM

Most of us want to do our best in areas important to us. Diligence and the willingness to work to achieve our goals are important character traits. But the desire to accomplish and please ourselves, others, and God can slip into perfectionism.

Perfectionism is based on a fear of not being good enough—fear that you will not be accepted (hired, liked, loved, admired, respected, approved of, etc.) unless you behave/perform/achieve perfectly. Perfectionism creates pressure and stress because of the person's inner need for acceptance and unrealistic expectations.

When you write messages, you may notice your perfectionist tendencies. If you give in to them, you can become overwhelmed and not able to finish the message. Or you may have perfectionist expectations of how you deliver the message.

How Can You Step Away From Perfectionism?

Receive God's unconditional love. He loves you just the way you are. He loves you whether people are impressed with you or not. Meditate on Scriptures that tell how much He loves you. Learn to write your messages and preach in God's strength. Turn it all over to Him and rest peacefully in His provision. Reach for excellence, but let go of perfectionism.

FEAR-REDUCTION TECHNIQUE #11
WATCH OUT FOR ASSUMPTIONS

We go through life noticing people and making assumptions about them. We assume something is true. We interpret what we see and make up stories that may or may not be correct.

Body Language Training

Several years ago in certain business circles, speakers and leaders were trained to make assumptions about other people based upon their body language. For example, crossed arms and crossed legs supposedly meant the person was shut down and resistant.

Be wary of this type of assumption. If someone is sitting with her arms crossed, maybe she is cold or has a stomachache. If a person is frowning, don't assume he does not like your message. Maybe he has a headache or family worries. If people get up and leave during your message, don't assume they disagree with you. There are many reasons why they might leave.

Notice Your Assumptions

If a person in the audience is older than you and dressed like a business executive, does your nervousness increase? If a famous Bible teacher is in the audience, does your fear level rise? Why? What assumptions are you making that feed your fears?

To reduce stress created by negative assumptions, do these things:

1. Don't jump to conclusions.
2. Notice your assumptions and toss them out.
3. Tell your brain, *Maybe that assumption is true, and maybe it's not.*
4. Don't interpret, because you don't really know.
5. Stay focused on delivering God's message.

FEAR-REDUCTION TECHNIQUE #12
PRETEND YOU ARE ANSWERING A QUESTION

You can pretend an audience member asked you a question. Your message is the answer. Think about it. Your message meets a need. It answers the questions of *what* to do, *when* to do it, *how* to do it, *where* to do it, and *why* a person should do it.

Some preachers create a question format for the audience. The speaker might say, "In your mind you may be saying, *How can I be loving toward people who are mean to me?* I'm glad you asked. Let's take a look at what God suggests in His Word."

Identify what question you are answering. For some people, it seems less stressful to answer a question than to deliver a message.

FEAR-REDUCTION TECHNIQUE #13
THINK ABOUT THE PEOPLE, THEIR NEEDS, AND GOD'S ANSWER TO THOSE NEEDS

Look at preaching from this perspective: Every human needs God's help. No matter what their social standing, job title, age, education level, gender, religion, or financial status, they all need God's help.

Are you God's minister? When you look at the audience, remember you are looking at individuals who need help. God wants to help them. He needs your help. They need your help. Help them.

If you are afraid of them, you cannot help them. If you are wrapped up in yourself, you cannot help them. If you will see the audience as individuals who need God's help and who are not superior to you, you can step away from fear. Get your thinking off yourself and onto the people, their needs, and God's answer to those needs.

FEAR-REDUCTION TECHNIQUE #14
PRAISE GOD

What is the opposite of fear? Faith and trust. What action shows faith and trust in God? Praise.

Before you get what you want, praise God. Praise Him ahead of time for working through you. Praise Him for strengthening you to do His work. Praise Him for helping you stay away from pride or confusion. Praise Him for giving you the right word at the right time. Praise Him for making people receptive to your message. Praise Him for the opportunity to serve. Praising God will build your confidence and reduce your fear.

FEAR-REDUCTION TECHNIQUE #15
USE SPIRITUAL WEAPONS

In the supernatural realm, there are forces that may try to come against you. Fear is one of them. When fear is a spiritual attack, deal with it spiritually. Through the LORDship of Jesus Christ, you have authority over negative forces. *"Behold, I give unto you power to tread on serpents and scorpions, and over all the power of the enemy: and nothing shall by any means hurt you"* (Luke 10:19). You have the power to trample fear under your feet.

The key is to step forward boldly and deal with it out loud. The volume does not matter. You can speak at a whisper and be successful. Confess fear as sin and ask God to forgive you. Renounce the fear, refuse to agree with it, and command it to go. Then thank God and speak a Scripture.

You could say something like this:

Father God, I confess I have sinned by thinking fear thoughts. I turn away from them. I ask You to forgive me and cleanse me. I thank You that You do (1 John 1:9). Fear, I renounce you! I refuse to think fear thoughts. God has not given me a spirit of fear, but of power, love, and a sound mind (2 Timothy 1:7). In the name of Jesus Christ of Nazareth, spirit of fear, I command you to go! It is written, Submit to God. Resist the devil and he will flee from you (James 4:7). So Fear, you have to flee. Get out now! Thank You, Father, for delivering me from fear.

Fear gives you an excellent opportunity to develop and build your faith.

FEAR-REDUCTION TECHNIQUE #16
FIND SCRIPTURE THAT WILL STRENGTHEN YOU

The Word is alive and powerful. Find Scriptures that will empower you to stand against fear.

- *"I can do all things through Christ which strengtheneth me"* (Philippians 4:13).
- *"For God hath not given us the spirit of fear; but of power, and of love, and of a sound mind"* (2 Timothy 1:7).
- *"What time I am afraid, I will trust in thee. In God I will praise his word, in God I have put my trust; I will not fear what flesh can do unto me"* (Psalm 56:3–4).
- *"For I the LORD thy God will hold thy right hand, saying unto thee, Fear not; I will help thee"* (Isaiah 41:13).

FEAR-REDUCTION TECHNIQUE #17
SEE PEOPLE THROUGH GOD'S EYES

When God looks at us, He is looking at His beloved children. No matter how many mistakes we have made or how many sins we have committed,

God loves us. He knows our weaknesses and our needs, but those things do not diminish our worth in His eyes. We are valuable and precious to Him. He sees us through the eyes of compassion. He knows when we are hurt, and He is touched by our pain and difficulty.

You can reduce or eliminate your fear if you will see the audience through God's eyes.

- See their value and their worth.
- Love them. Let them be precious to you.
- See their problems, hurts, and confusion.
- Let your heart be moved by their pain.
- Feel the heart of Jesus longing to set them free.

Seeing people through God's eyes gets you out of your own way. Then you can deliver the life-changing Word of God.

FEAR-REDUCTION TECHNIQUE #18
BREATHE DEEPLY AND SPEAK YOUR FAITH

This breathing exercise combines all three areas (mental, physical, and spiritual) into one application. As you take a deep breath, say, "I breathe deeply and relax because_____." (Finish the sentence with a Scriptural statement.)

- "I breathe deeply and relax because God is with me."
- "I breathe deeply and relax because You gird me with strength and make my way perfect."

Note: Many people try to fight their battles silently in the mental realm. That is not an effective strategy. If you don't speak, you can easily lose the battle. But if you step into the faith realm and speak words of faith, you position yourself for God to turn your situation around.

FEAR-REDUCTION TECHNIQUE #19
ACCEPT GOD'S LOVE:
PERFECT LOVE CASTS OUT FEAR

There is no fear in love; but perfect love casteth out fear. (1 John 4:18)

1. Realize God loves you totally and completely. His love is not based on your ability to preach or on your good works. It is not based on your being perfect. Choose to believe and receive His amazing love. It will give you inner confidence. It will strengthen and stabilize you.

2. You can decide to love each of your listeners. The love you have for them can balance you and kick out fear.

3. I know a preacher who also decides that his listeners love him. He says it helps him stay calm.

FEAR-REDUCTION TECHNIQUE #20
BE BOLD

It's easy to cave in to thoughts of inadequacy and insecurity. It's tempting to feel intimidated. Someone in your audience may know the Bible better, have a deeper revelation, or be a better speaker than you. He may have a stronger anointing and have better education than you. Someone may criticize you, disagree with you, or dislike you. There are many thoughts with which you can intimidate yourself. Toss them out.

Pray for boldness and ask your friends to pray for boldness for you (just like Paul did in Ephesians 6:18–20). Your belief in the Word brings confidence and transfers authority to you. Preach the Bible as the true and living Word that it is. Be bold!

FEAR-REDUCTION TECHNIQUE #21
TRUST GOD

Thou wilt keep him in perfect peace, whose mind is stayed on thee: because he trusteth in thee. Trust ye in the Lord for ever: for in the Lord JEHOVAH is everlasting strength. (Isaiah 26:3–4)

Did God call you to preach and speak for Him? Did He ask you to be a co-laborer with Him? Is He your shield, your fortress, your place of protection? Is He your deliverer and comforter? Did He promise to never leave you nor forsake you?

Trust God to be Who He says He is and to do what He says He will do. His strength is made perfect in your weakness. Cast your cares on the Lord and trust Him to lead you, guide you, and work through you. He needs you, and you need Him. It's a perfect combination.

God will honor your faith in Him. His grace will be sufficient for you. So take Him at His Word (trust Him) and let your heart be at peace.

CHAPTER 11

HOW TO MANAGE FEAR SYMPTOMS DURING THE MESSAGE

When Kate McVeigh was in high school, she was so terrified of speaking publicly that she fainted when she stood up to do book reports.[1] Today, many years later, she is a confident and effective traveling minister who even preaches on television and radio. No matter how bad your stage-fright symptoms are, you can learn to overcome them and do what God has called you to do.

Physical anxiety symptoms are not fun. If your legs, arms, hands, knees, jaw, or mouth tremble and shake and your voice is tremulous and weak, it can be disconcerting. You need to know what to do if that happens.

Tense and Release

If you are waiting to speak and your body feels tense or is trembling, inconspicuously tense and release some of your muscles. If there is a way to tense your hand into a fist and then relax it or shake your fingers (without being noticed), that can help.

HOW TO MANAGE PHYSICAL FEAR SYMPTOMS *DURING* THE MESSAGE

First of all, don't tell the audience you are nervous or frightened. If you do, it will increase your nervousness, undermine your leadership, distract people from hearing your message, and cause some members of the audience to worry about you.

Most Important Tip

For a problem with trembling or shaking, *move the muscles involved.* Trembling and shakiness is a sign of too much energy. Get rid of it by moving. Lean forward, take some steps, or make a large arm movement.

Let's look now at specific situations. What should you do for the following conditions?

Tickle in Your Throat

1. Cough away from the microphone.
2. Drink water.
3. Have cough drops available.

Perspiring Face

1. Use a handkerchief or small towel to wipe your face.
2. Don't let it distract you. Just wipe and get on with your message.

Mispronounced Words

1. Slow down.
2. If it was minor, continue speaking at a slower pace. Don't point it out or try to make a joke of it.
3. If it was major, correct it. If it was funny, you can correct it and laugh. But don't make a big deal out of it. Don't stick out your tongue and say, "Blah! I can't even talk today."
4. Pause to collect yourself; then continue.
5. Don't get embarrassed. Don't let a mispronunciation distract you.

Memory Problem

1. Bring a written form of the message with major points highlighted in yellow: (a) a word-for-word manuscript, or (b) an outline, or (c) note cards, numbered in sequence.
2. Breathe deeply to keep oxygen coming to your brain.
3. Stay focused and in the moment.

4. If you blank out you can say, "My brain just went somewhere else. What were we talking about?" "Oh, thank you. Yes."
5. You may need to stay at the lectern with your finger on the outline, touching where you are in the message as you speak.

Memory trick: In your practice time, link the ending of one section or story with the beginning of the next section. Train your mind to see the two connected.

Dry Mouth

1. Pause and intensify eye contact.[2]
2. Sip water.
3. Run your tongue inconspicuously along the inside back of your lower front teeth (with your mouth closed).
4. A small mint in the side of your cheek is an option, but it can distract both you and the audience.

Note: Caffeine dehydrates. It will dry out your mouth. Don't consume anything with caffeine in it on the day you preach.

Shaky Hands

1. Make a large arm gesture.
2. Move your body (i.e., take steps, move your feet, or lean forward).
3. Don't hold things that rattle. (Papers rattle; note cards do not.)

Pounding Heart

1. Make eye contact with someone.
2. Breathe deeply.
3. Silently say to yourself, "I'm fine. Heart, be calm."

Quivery Voice

1. Make eye contact. Focus on the audience and their needs.

2. Pause.
3. Lower your pitch.[3]
4. Speak slower.
5. Enunciate carefully.
6. If this happens to you regularly, take preventative action by doing a Before-Speaking Routine: yawn, hum, make funny faces, etc., in private before you speak.

Voice Too Quiet

1. Open your mouth wider while you speak.
2. Breathe deeply, inconspicuously.
3. Stand on both feet. Do not sit.
4. Keep your chest lifted, your head up, and your shoulders back.
5. Make an effort to project your voice to the back row of your audience.

Embarrassment

Usually the only time the audience becomes embarrassed is if you get embarrassed. Decide ahead of time you will not be embarrassed by a mistake. Refuse to feel stupid.

Note: The previous subheadings (except for the last two), along with the endnote items, came from Joan Detz in her books *How to Write and Give a Speech* and *Can You Say a Few Words?*

If you are called to preach, be tenacious. No matter how severe your physical or emotional fear symptoms may be, you can overcome them and do what God has called you to do. He will honor your heart's desire to serve Him and empower you to preach. So be bold. Don't yield to intimidation. You have a job to do, and God is big enough and faithful enough to provide you with His strength. No matter what fear symptoms show up, go ahead and preach.

CHAPTER 12

CONFIDENCE AND THE PERCEPTION OF CONFIDENCE

Did you ever see former U.S. president Ronald Reagan speak? He exuded confidence, warmth, and good humor. He gave us the impression he was comfortable talking to anyone—and that he was pleasantly in charge. Some people called him the "Great Communicator."

John C. Maxwell, in his book *Be a People Person*, says, "If there is one quality you could have that would make you successful in motivating people or convincing people to follow your lead, that trait would be confidence."[1]

HOW DOES A SPEAKER DEVELOP CONFIDENCE?

It helps to develop positive attitudes and have positive speaking experiences.

Develop Positive Speaking Attitudes

When you notice a negative thought about your speaking ability, you can say, "I refuse to believe that thought. It is not correct. In fact, this is what I believe..." Then speak a positive statement.

Create Positive Speaking Experiences

1. Know your message. If you know the message, confidence will develop naturally as you speak with authority and conviction.

2. Speak publicly as often as you can. Look for opportunities. Some preachers start by speaking on street corners. Ask the Holy Spirit to show you where He wants you to speak.

3. Speech training can create confidence. Consider taking a speech class, working with a public-speaking coach, or joining a public-speaking group.

THE PERCEPTION OF CONFIDENCE

Audiences tend to relax and are more receptive when the speaker appears confident. For the audience's comfort, it is the *perception* of confidence that matters. If you are not confident but appear to be, it will help the audience receive your message. So the question becomes, what can help nervous speakers look as if they are confident?

Audience members will notice your posture, walk, movements, vocal quality, facial expressions, energy levels, warmth (or lack of it), and mood. Follow these suggestions if you want to be perceived as being confident:

1. Use excellent posture. Stand up straight. Keep your head up.
2. Walk with a confident stride.
3. Make eye contact with people.
4. Smile.
5. Warm up your voice ahead of time so your voice does not crack.
6. Warm up your body ahead of time so your movements are not stiff.
7. Don't speak too fast. Rushing through a message can give the impression you are nervous.
8. Use pauses effectively.
9. Present an organized, easy-to-understand message.
10. Tell your listeners the benefits of applying the message to their lives.

11. Show them how to apply the message and encourage them to do it.
12. Speak with authority, sincerity, and conviction.

REASONS FOR AUTHENTIC CONFIDENCE

Your authentic confidence comes from your faith in God. When you believe the Bible is the inspired, inerrant Word of God, you have your solid Rock to stand on. You can then preach with authority, and confidence is not just a good outward show. Even as a beginning preacher, authority and confidence can exude from you because you know you are a child of the King, called to preach, a co-laborer with God, equipped, emboldened, and strengthened by Him.

SECTION III

LONG-TERM PREPARATION

INTRODUCTION

Speaking for God requires preparation and prayer. We have already noted several areas of long-term preparation: learning to connect with your listeners, building your credibility as a preacher, learning fear-reduction techniques, learning about the anointing, and developing godly character traits. In this *Long-Term Preparation* section, we touch on four more areas of preparation.

If you follow the recommendations in this section, you can keep yourself healthier and physically stronger, eliminate misunderstandings if you are a traveling preacher, discover the needs of your audience, avoid embarrassing physical and emotional habits, and set the foundation for an anointed message through prayer. There is no substitute for the right kind of preparation and fervent prayer.

CHAPTER 13

TAKE CARE OF THE TEMPLE OF GOD

Know ye not that ye are the temple of God, and that the Spirit of God dwelleth in you? If any man defile the temple of God, him shall God destroy; for the temple of God is holy, which temple ye are. (1 Corinthians 3:16–17)

We work hard to take care of our church buildings. We keep them clean, beautiful, and functional. If a leak develops, we repair it. But better than repairing a leak is to prevent it. Sometimes we take care of everything except our own bodies. We only have one body in this life. If we don't take care of it, we can end up sick and limited in our ability to serve God. He expects us to be good caretakers of our bodies.

NUTRITION

Long-Term Nutrition

Public speaking and ministering take energy. Some ministers burn out or become sick and leave the ministry. Your choice of foods, the time you eat, and the amount you eat will affect your ability to maintain health in the midst of a demanding work schedule.

Your body needs the right kind of fuel. We don't put kerosene in our cars. That is the wrong fuel. One minister I know of eliminated coffee from his diet after thirty years of heavy coffee consumption. He said the LORD told him it would ruin his health if he continued drinking it. Another minister cut out all cola drinks and chocolate from his diet—also for the same reason. Our bodies were designed to function at peak performance when supplied with pure air, clean water, adequate rest, exercise, and healthy food.

Nutrition on the Day of the Message

Pay attention to your nutritional needs. It is your job to know how you function best and to provide the optimal conditions.

Some speakers never eat before they speak. Others eat only lightly, but some can eat right before the message and have no problem. Learn what works for you regarding food. I never eat right before speaking. I think better if I eat protein and fat, but it has to be at least 30 minutes before the speech. It takes at least 20 minutes after I eat for my mouth to stop producing extra saliva (which gets in the way of accurate pronunciation). Also, my mind is not as sharp and clear when my body is beginning to digest food.

Food Recommendations Before Public Speaking

- Drink lots of water for forty-eight hours before you speak.
- Avoid caffeine: It is a dehydrator. It will dry out your throat and vocal cords. Also, it can make you jittery. Avoid coffee, tea, cola, chocolate, etc.
- Avoid carbonated beverages: They may make you burp.
- Avoid heavy meals: They may slow down your thinking ability and energy.
- Avoid simple carbohydrates like sugar or pasta: They can make you tired.

Plan ahead. If you need to eat before speaking, bring food with you. Sometimes people say, "We'll feed you" or "There will be plenty of time to go to a restaurant." But plans may change. Be ready with a back-up plan if the meal does not happen as promised.

SLEEP

Deep, sweet sleep is a gift of God. Without the right amount, we function at a disadvantage. Live a lifestyle where you get enough rest. And get a good night's sleep the night before you preach.

EXERCISE

Include regular exercise in your lifestyle. Being physically fit will help you present God's messages in more dynamic ways and help you stay healthy.

FORGIVENESS

When one of my pastors was a young minister, he went to a conference where a respected elderly preacher spoke. After the meeting, the young pastor asked, "Sir, what do I need to do to be successful in ministry?" The old man replied, "If you don't get bitter, you'll make it."

If you are a Christian leader, you will be criticized. You may be slandered. Untrue rumors may circulate. No matter how badly you get hurt, forgive and pray for those who harmed you. The Lord tells us to do this because He is trying to protect us. If you don't obey, it can keep your prayers from being answered, block your anointing, keep you from hearing the voice of God, and make your body sick. God has a job for you. He needs you to be well.

CASTING YOUR CARES ON THE LORD

Humble yourselves therefore under the mighty hand of God, that he may exalt you in due time: Casting all your care upon him; for he careth for you. (1 Peter 5:6–7)

Life situations are rarely perfect. We may be overworked and too busy. We may struggle with depression or a broken heart. We may have a parent with Alzheimer's disease, a disabled child, financial problems, personal illness—the list is endless. Worry, stress, and fears knock at our door.

Stress is a major challenge. In his book *The Bible Cure for Stress*, Dr. Don Colbert quotes these statistics:

- 43% of all adults suffer adverse health effects due to stress.
- 75% to 90% of all visits to primary care physicians are for stress-related complaints or disorders.
- Chronic stress has been linked to most of the leading causes of death.[1]

The LORD does not want us weighed down. We either cast our cares on the LORD, or we pay the price. Serving God is easier when we do what He says. A surrendered life to God includes not worrying. We will be more effective ministers if we give our burdens to the LORD.

BEING LED BY THE SPIRIT OF GOD

In order to do God's work and live a victorious life, we need to develop our ability to detect His guidance. As we mature in our relationship with the LORD, we become increasingly capable of hearing His voice and knowing what He wants us to do.

How Does God Lead Us?

God speaks to us in different ways at different times. Often He speaks through the Bible as we read it or mull it over. He may lead us to a Scripture that is perfect for our situation. Sometimes the LORD speaks in a still, small voice in our spirit.

He may give us a dream or vision. He may give us a feeling of peace or a lack of peace. Sometimes He leads us by our desires. Occasionally He speaks to certain ministers in an audible voice. But much of the time, He speaks to us through our intuition. At those times, we just *know* what is right and what we are to do or not do.

Why is the topic of being led by the Spirit found in this chapter on taking care of the temple of God? Your ability to follow the lead of the Holy Spirit may mean the difference between life and death.

God Leads Us by Our Intuition

I heard Kenneth E. Hagin, the founder of Rhema Bible Training College, tell this story: He had just taught on being led by the Spirit of God by paying attention to your intuition. After his message, a pastor came up to him and told him the following story: The pastor said he had been in three major car accidents. All three times, he had sensed beforehand that he was not supposed to leave on time. He had an inner urging that indicated he should wait thirty minutes. But all three times, he discounted the feeling and left on schedule. Each time resulted in an accident with injuries. And in the last accident, his wife was killed.[2] If this pastor had realized his intuitional feeling was the Spirit of God trying to guide him, his wife's life could have been spared.

A member of my church arranged to go on a short-term mission trip to Asia. A few days before her departure date, she sensed she was not supposed to go. She cancelled her flight and lost $200 in the process. Only one day after her scheduled arrival date in Asia, a tsunami hit, killing almost everyone in the area where she would have been.

I can think of five times God saved my life when I followed my intuition. In the moment, I did not know it was the Holy Spirit leading me. I just knew what I needed to do, and I did it. But I also remember when I ignored an intuitional leading. I let my mind talk me out of it. As a result, I fell and injured my wrist and face. It took a year to recover.

Evangelist Billy Graham told this story of following his intuition: He and his ministry team returned to their hotel after a meeting. He sensed something was wrong and that he should not be the first person to step into his hotel room. He asked one of the men with him to open the door and go in first. When his associate stepped into the room, a woman threw herself into his arms and kissed him. At the same time, camera flash bulbs went off, capturing a picture of the moment.[3]

The Holy Spirit is ever present, seeking to avert situations that could harm you or your ministry. If you are sensitive to His leading, He can protect you.

God May Lead You Through Words or Thoughts

David Beebe, one of my teachers at Rhema Bible Training College, told us that when he was a pastor, a person in his church asked him to visit a sick man in the hospital. Pastor Beebe was getting ready to go out of town to a conference, so he decided to visit the man after he returned.

As he ran errands, getting ready to leave town, he passed the hospital. He heard in his spirit, "Why don't you just go and do that now?" But he did not do it. An hour later, he passed the hospital again and heard the same thing, "Why don't you just go and do that now?" But again, he continued on his errands. After a couple more hours, he passed the hospital a third time and heard the same words. This time he took note. He stopped at the hospital and visited with the man. After Pastor Beebe explained the plan of salvation, the man accepted Jesus. Pastor Beebe said, "I'm going out of town to a conference. I'll see you when I get back."

When Pastor Beebe returned, he learned the man had died three hours after their conversation.[4] Remembering this story helps me pay attention to possible Holy Spirit guidance through words or thoughts I might otherwise ignore.

In a less dramatic way, I sometimes respond to words that I absent-mindedly hear myself mutter, like, "Get that letter written, Pam, before the timing is wrong." Or, "Take care of that. You're wasting energy by putting it off."

Don't discount your intuition, words you hear in your spirit, or what you notice yourself thinking or saying. Let the Holy Spirit lead you.

CHAPTER 14

PRELIMINARY RESEARCH

As I sat in a chapel meeting, I realized the main speaker was beginning her conclusion after speaking for only thirteen minutes. I thought to myself, *Uh-oh, didn't the meeting planner tell her she was to speak for forty-five minutes?* Apparently not, because at the fifteen minute mark, the speaker ended her talk.

The meeting planner whispered to me, "We need a thirty minute message. I don't have anything. Do you?"

"Yes," I replied and walked up to the lectern and preached for the remaining thirty minutes.

How could the miscommunication between the original speaker and the meeting planner have been prevented? The following research will help you avoid misunderstandings and incorrect assumptions.

INTERVIEW THE MEETING PLANNER

Unless you are the pastor of the church where you are speaking, someone invited you to speak. I call that person the meeting planner.

Ask him (or her) to clarify the following situations:

1. Amount of time for delivery of your message
2. Date and time of service and expected arrival time
3. Location (including address)
4. Possible topics for the message

5. Person who will do the altar call
6. Bible translation the pastor uses
7. Special challenges the congregation is facing
8. Makeup of the audience: age, gender ratio, language and dialects they speak, number of people expected, special focus groups (are they all missionaries, recovering addicts, etc.)
9. Description of the meeting room and the layout: If you plan to use audio-visual equipment, can the lights be dimmed? Is there a lectern? Does it have a light? Is there a spare bulb available? Is there a shelf under the lectern where you can put things?
10. Sound system and type of microphone
11. Video and audio recording agreement
12. Types of support personnel available: ushers, sound-system persons, volunteers to sell your products, etc.
13. Materials you will need them to provide: i.e., lectern, microphone, table set-up to sell your products, volunteers to work at the table, glass of water, etc.
14. Order of the service: what will happen and when
15. Person who will introduce you
16. Housing arrangements
17. Financial arrangements
18. Name and contact information of church leaders and meeting planner
19. Name and contact information of person who will greet you or pick you up at the airport
20. Ask, "Is there anything else I should know?"

VERIFY THE AGREEMENT IN WRITING

A person I knew from Bible school traveled with a youth ministry team across the United States to their ministry destination in California. The head of their ministry had arranged for them to lead praise and worship in various churches along the way in exchange for a share of the offering and a place to sleep.

At one of the churches, the senior pastor (who had agreed to their coming) had gone out of town. The associate pastor was in charge, but during praise and worship he kept saying to them, "Not yet." Finally, he invited them to join the church musicians on the last song. No share of the offering was given to them.

A church family had agreed to have them stay in their home overnight. When the ministry team got to the house, they were offered one bedroom with a double bed for the four of them. The person who told me this story said she slept in her clothing on the floor with no pillow or blanket.

This story is a classic example of what can happen when agreements are not clearly communicated. Professional speakers put all agreements in writing and obtain the necessary signatures. As a minister, you will not have an extensive written agreement like a professional speaker has, but it helps to get something in writing to clarify the main details.

At the very least, you should send a letter of agreement or email for their confirmation. You may find that people change their minds when they see in writing what you have previously discussed. That's fine. I am not recommending you try to tie people into agreements they don't want. I am suggesting that a written agreement helps all parties avoid confusion and offense.

Note: A friend of mine who is a traveling minister disagrees with me. She and her husband prefer to communicate only verbally with the pastors who invite them to preach. You will need to decide what works best for you.

CHAPTER 15

IDENTIFY YOUR HABITS

Once, in the middle of presenting a six-hour seminar, I realized I had just put the knuckle of my right index finger up to my nose to wipe the slight drip. At that moment, I became aware that it was a habit and that I had done it probably three times during the presentation.

In his book *The Anatomy of Preaching*, David L. Larsen states:

> Every preacher should be videotaped every few years for a critique of form and silly habits that can obtrude. I recall a professor who helped me greatly by pointing out that I launched the sermon with an elevation of my nostrils like a bull pawing the ground. It was a gesture of arrogance and needed prompt attention.[1]

Everyone has physical, mental, emotional, and vocal habits. You might be surprised to see yourself on a TV screen doing things you are not aware that you do. Develop self-awareness. Work to identify your habits. It can save you embarrassment.

PHYSICAL HABITS

You need to avoid some physical habits while you minister. I know several people who are unconscious scratchers. While talking, they scratch their face, head, neck, arms, or stomach—seemingly without being aware of it. They may even reach underneath their clothing to scratch an itch. Don't let that be you.

Are any of these among your habits? Do you raise your eyebrows? Roll your eyes? Purse your lips while you think? Wrinkle your nose? Frown? Adjust your clothing? Run your fingers through your hair? Point your index finger at people? Stick your tongue out when you pause or laugh? Lick your lips repetitively?

Become aware of your physical habits. Avoid those that might be distracting to your audience.

VOCAL HABITS

What sounds do you habitually make? Do you sigh, yawn out loud, or sneeze loudly? Make unusual sounds with your mouth? Speak in a monotone? Giggle or laugh a lot? Speak with curt and abrupt words? Speak too loudly or softly? Whistle through your teeth? Clear your throat often?

Several years ago, I picked up the habit of using the word "man" as an exclamation. I had a friend who would say, "Man, that was a good movie! Oh man, did you see that?" After hearing the expression repeatedly, it slipped into my speech pattern. It took work to eliminate the habit.

EMOTIONAL HABITS

Our emotional habits can slip into our presentations without our awareness. I have seen preachers become annoyed or antagonistic when they were not pleased with the audience. Some showed it in their tone of voice. Others became sarcastic.

Think about your emotional habits. If someone disagrees with you or does not view you as an authority, are you threatened or insulted? If people don't appreciate your hard work, do you get resentful? If someone criticizes you, do you become defensive?

Some people get angry when they're afraid. Others laugh or giggle when they are frightened, nervous, or don't know what to do. During public-speaking training with a group of worship-leader students, one of the young women could not stop laughing when it was her turn to carry out the speaking exercise in front of the class. I used Fear-Reduction Technique #17 (See People through God's Eyes) to help her vault beyond her fear-based behavior.

What emotional behavior is among your habits? What do you do when you are nervous or uncomfortable? Do you talk faster or avoid eye contact? Does your posture change? When you are tired or under pressure, what negative state might you slip into? Discouragement? Self-pity? Anxiety? When you are confident and happy, how do you behave?

If a comedian were to mimic you, what would he do? What posture, tone of voice, mental outlook, emotion, and verbal expression would he use? Self-knowledge gives you the ability to choose your best components for your presentations. Ignorance of personal habits can undercut your messages.

CHAPTER 16

PRAYERS BEFORE PREACHING

Praying always with all prayer and supplication in the Spirit, and watching thereunto with all perseverance and supplication for all saints; and for me, that utterance may be given unto me, that I may open my mouth boldly, to make known the mystery of the gospel. (Ephesians 6:18-19)

There is no way we can overemphasize the importance of prayer. It is the foundation for effective ministry. In the book *Why God Used D. L. Moody*, R. A. Torrey writes, "The second secret of the great power exhibited in Mr. Moody's life was that *Mr. Moody was in the deepest and most meaningful sense a man of prayer*... [he] was the most wonderful preacher I have ever heard... but out of a very intimate acquaintance with him I wish to testify that he was a far greater *pray-er* than he was a preacher."[1]

Charles Spurgeon said, "Never account prayer second to preaching."[2] He also said, "I have not preached this morning half as much as I have prayed. For every word that I have spoken, I have prayed two words silently to God."[3]

When you are invited to speak, pray about whether to accept the invitation. If God answers yes, pray for the church and pastor. Ask the Lord to tell you what they need. Then do your research and pray for the anointing to write and deliver the message. Pray that the listeners will be open and receptive. Establish a habit of daily prayer and dedicate your work to God.

RELATIONSHIP WITH GOD

Read your Bible. Spend time in God's presence. Talk with Him, listen to Him, and worship Him. Don't let your ministry duties or message preparation take the place of your time with the LORD. Charles Spurgeon said, "Above all, feed the flame with intimate fellowship with Christ."[4]

In his book *My Utmost for His Highest*, Oswald Chambers comments, "The bearing of fruit is always shown in Scripture to be the visible result of an intimate relationship with Jesus Christ (see John 15:1–4)."[5]

FASTING AND PRAYER

Some ministers regularly fast and pray; others do not. There are times when fasting and prayer is the best thing to do.

Often when D. L. Moody, the evangelist and founder of Moody Bible Institute, was about to start some new work, he would write to R. A. Torrey and ask him to have the ministry students fast and pray. R. A. Torrey writes:

> Often we were gathered in the lecture room far into the night—sometimes till one, two, three, four or even five o'clock in the morning, crying to God, just because Mr. Moody urged us to wait upon God until we received His blessing. How many men and women I have known whose lives and characters have been transformed by those nights of prayer and who have wrought mighty things in many lands because of those nights of prayer![6]

INTERCESSORY PRAYERS

In some churches, a prayer group meets an hour before each service to pray. Large churches often have intercessory prayer teams praying many hours a week—sometimes twenty-four hours a day. In his book *The Anatomy of Preaching*, David L. Larsen tells the following story.

> Charles Haddon Spurgeon attributed the signal blessing of God upon his ministry in London to the faithfulness of his people

to pray for him. The story has often been told of the five college students who came to hear Spurgeon preach at the Metropolitan Tabernacle. While waiting for the doors to open, they were greeted by a gentleman who offered to show them around. "Would you like to see the heating plant?" he inquired. They were not particularly interested because it was a hot day in July. Nonetheless they followed him down a staircase where he opened a door, whispering: "This is our heating plant." The surprised students saw seven hundred people bowed in prayer, interceding for the service about to begin upstairs and for their beloved pastor. Softly closing the door, the gentleman then introduced himself to them. It was Spurgeon.[7]

Regarding the 4,000 decisions for Christ after he preached in Madras, India, Billy Graham said, "Such a result witnessed to the spiritual power generated by the twenty-four-hour prayer chains that had preceded our visit."[8] Find people of prayer to intercede for you. Ask them to pray before and during your message.

PRAYING SCRIPTURE OVER YOURSELF

Find a Scripture that matches your situation and personalize it. Claim it as your own. Believe it and speak it. For example, "Lord, I thank You that in Exodus 4:12 You said, '*Now therefore go, and I will be with thy mouth, and teach thee what thou shalt say.*' Lord, those words are for me. I only want to say what You want me to say, and I thank You that You will provide the words."

When you pray Scripture over yourself, it puts you into the faith realm. God is no respecter of persons, but He is a respecter of faith. He looks for people who are acting in faith. When Keith Moore ran the healing school at Rhema Bible Training College, he would pray and meditate on Isaiah 61:1–4 for forty-five minutes before he went out to minister. As he meditated on the Scripture, he personalized it, speaking it as reality for his own ministry. He would say, "*The Spirit of the Lord God is upon **me**; because the Lord has anointed **me** to preach good tidings unto the meek…*" When he did that, he said the healing anointing upon him was much stronger.[9]

HOLY SPIRIT-WRITTEN PRAYERS

No matter what you need, the Holy Spirit-written prayers in Ephesians and Colossians can move you toward victory (Ephesians 1:17–23; Ephesians 3:11–12, 14–21; Colossians 1:9–14). Pray over yourself a personalized version of these prayers. Replace "you" with "me," "your" with "my," etc. You might start with a statement like, "Father I thank You for this Holy Spirit-written prayer. I know it is Your will for me, so I pray it over myself right now."

Example: Personalized Version of Ephesians 3:11–12, 14–21 Prayer

> [11] **Dear Father,** According to the eternal purpose which **You** purposed in Christ Jesus our Lord: [12] In whom we have boldness and access with confidence by the faith of him. [14] For this cause I bow my knees unto **You,** the Father of our Lord Jesus Christ, [15] Of whom the whole family in heaven and earth is named, [16] That **You** would grant **me**, according to the riches of **Your** glory, to be strengthened with might by **Your** Spirit in **my** inner man; [17] That Christ may dwell in **my** heart by faith; that **I**, being rooted and grounded in love, [18] May be able to comprehend with all saints what is the breadth, and length, and depth, and height; [19] And to know the love of Christ, which passeth knowledge, that **I** might be filled with all the fulness of God. [20] Now unto **You** who is able to do exceeding abundantly above all that **I** ask or think, according to the power that worketh in **me**, [21] Unto **You** be glory in the church by Christ Jesus throughout all ages, world without end. Amen.

PRAYING ALOUD IN THE PULPIT AT THE BEGINNING OF THE MESSAGE

When you listen to preachers, notice whether they start in prayer or not. If you begin with prayer, it can unify the listeners and make your preaching more effective. It moves things in the spiritual realm.

Example of an opening prayer:

Father, we thank You for Your love, for Your Son Jesus, and for the ability to come together to worship and learn about You. I ask You to give me the ability to speak Your message in the way You want it spoken. Help all people who hear this message to receive what You have for them. In the name of Jesus, I break the power of anything that would try to hinder the understanding and acceptance of God's message. I break the power of all distractions in the name of Jesus, Amen.

Every denomination seems to have its own style of prayer. Some prayers are long and intense. Others may be brief and sound casual. The length and style don't matter. The important thing is that the prayer is sincere, speaks to a current need, is spoken in faith, and is Scriptural.

Sometimes the minister who opens the service prays aloud from the lectern. If this is the case, you might decide not to open in prayer. If you are not going to pray at the beginning, pray beforehand to break the power of all distractions.

There is no substitute for submitted, worshipful prayer in your lifestyle. The power that you experience as you preach will be a reflection of your prayer life and your obedience. Keeping your relationship with God vibrant is like putting top quality gasoline into a racecar.

SECTION IV

WRITING THE MESSAGE

INTRODUCTION

Some preachers need more help writing the message than delivering it. For others, it is the reverse. Writing messages requires talent, knowledge, and godly inspiration. It is also a skill that is developed with practice.

In this *Writing the Message* section, you will discover the secrets of great orators and highly effective preachers. You will find specific tools to help you organize your thoughts and illustrate concepts so your teaching stays in your listener's memory.

As you learn to use these tools, message writing will become easier and start to come naturally to you.

CHAPTER 17

FOLLOW BASIC MESSAGE GUIDELINES

These guidelines will help you write relevant, life-changing messages.

GUIDELINE #1: WRITE SIMPLE, WELL-ORGANIZED MESSAGES

- To develop this ability, go preach to children. That will force you to communicate with basic words and concepts.
- Some instructors of preaching recommend you write your messages word for word for the first two years of your ministry. That will help you develop the discipline and skill of writing organized messages.

GUIDELINE #2: MAKE THE MESSAGE SCRIPTURAL

In his book *Why God Used D. L. Moody*, R. A. Torrey states:

> Oh, men and women, if you wish to get an audience and wish to do that audience some good after you get them, *study*, study, STUDY the one Book, *preach*, preach, PREACH the one Book, *teach*, teach, TEACH the one Book, the Bible, the only Book that contains God's Word, and the only Book that has power to gather and hold and bless the crowds.[1]

In 2 Timothy 4:2, Paul says, "*Preach the word.*" In order to make your message Scriptural, you need to research your chosen Scriptures.

1. Notice what the context is. What is the main theme of the book and chapter where your Scripture is located? What is the subject matter of surrounding verses? What point is the author making? Don't take your Scripture out of context. Study what comes before and after your Scripture so you don't mislead your listeners as to the meaning.

2. Who is the writer of the book? Who is the speaker? Who is he talking to? What is their situation?

3. Do word studies. Don't assume you know the meaning of words in your chosen Scripture. If you have the King James Version, you can use *The New Strong's Exhaustive Concordance of the Bible*, or *Vine's Complete Expository Dictionary of Old and New Testament Words*.

4. Take the Bible literally whenever possible, except when Scripture forces you not to—like when it is using similes, metaphors, poetry, imagery, etc.

5. Double reference: The rule of double reference allows us to apply Scripture to both Israel and to the church today (Christians) as the Spirit of God directs. Many Scriptures that are historical are also personal to us. They actually happened in history, but God is also speaking to us about our situation through them.

6. Comparison: Compare your verse with other verses that deal with the same subject. Don't create doctrine out of only one Scripture.

7. Look at different translations to see if your interpretation of Scripture matches.

8. What time period is your text in? Is it during the Mosaic covenant? Is it in the New Testament? Is it before the cross or after it?

Key Point: Show the listeners the exact Scripture you are preaching from. If you preach the ideas of the Bible without showing people the relevant text, you are asking them to view you as the authority. Instead, point them to God's Word as the authority.

Your job is to demonstrate that the Bible is an alive and active road map. It is our guide, our protection, and our wisdom. It is relevant to our daily lives, whether we are happy or sad, rich or poor, young or old. If we preach the Bible, we know we speak for God.

GUIDELINE #3: MEET PEOPLE'S NEEDS

Previously, we noted the importance of matching the message to a need the people have. That is how you make the message relevant to their lives.

GUIDELINE #4: DEMONSTRATE THE NEED

Your job is not only to address a need, but also to convince the audience they have the need. People already know they need food, clothing, and shelter. But spiritual needs are often not understood. Show your listeners why they need to forgive, pray, and develop their faith. When you present a salvation message, explain what they need to be saved from and why.

After you demonstrate to your listeners that they have a need, then you can show them God's plan to meet the need.

GUIDELINE #5: EXPLAIN THE BENEFITS OF APPLYING THE MESSAGE

In the realm of business, a good salesperson tells the benefits of his product. You are a salesperson for God. Explain His benefits. Through the psalmist, the Holy Spirit shows us the importance of knowing God's benefits. *"Bless the Lord, O my soul, and forget not all his benefits: Who forgiveth all thine iniquities; who healeth all thy diseases"* (Psalm 103:2–3). When you preach a salvation message, tell the benefits of getting saved. For a *Praising God* message, you could point out these benefits:

- God inhabits the praises of His people. (Psalm 22:3)
- If you praise and trust in Him, He will defend you. (Psalm 5:11)

- The power of praise will stop the enemy. (Psalm 8:2)
- Praising God positions you for deliverance. (Psalm 50:14–15, 23; Acts 16:25–26)

When you explain the benefits, you answer the listeners' questions of *How will this help me? What difference can this make in my life?*

GUIDELINE #6: EXPLAIN HOW TO APPLY THE MESSAGE

For a salvation message, you will tell how to be saved and give listeners the opportunity to make Jesus their Lord. For a forgiveness message, you will tell them what to do if they feel unable to forgive. And you will probably lead them in a forgiveness prayer.

If you preach a message on *Praising God* and recommend that your listeners increase their praise, you could show them Scriptural examples of the following:

- You can thank God for what He does. (Psalm 107:15)
    - » Thank God for forgiving, cleansing, and saving you.
    - » Thank God for protecting you.
    - » Thank God for loving you.
    - » Thank God for making you a new creation; you have personal access to Him; you are a child of God and a joint-heir with Christ.

- You can praise God for Who He is by describing Him.
    - » You are Lord of lords and King of kings.
    - » You are the magnificent Creator of heaven and earth.
    - » You are my Redeemer, Deliverer, and Healer.
    - » You are gracious and full of compassion.

- You can praise Him with a variety of activities.
    - » You can sing to Him. (Psalm 108:1)

- » You can dance for Him. (Psalm 149:3)
- » You can lift your hands to honor Him. (Psalm 134:2)
- » You can shout your praises. (Psalm 66:1)

The how-to-apply-the-message information is neglected by some preachers. I have seen heart-based, inspired preachers speak to a deep need in the listeners' lives, but then leave them with no way to satisfy the need.

In his book *The Anatomy of Preaching*, David L. Larsen says, "Many a sermon leaves us motivated to do something, whether serve or witness or hope or rejoice, but we are abandoned on the ropes because the 'how-to' step is missing."[3]

Showing the listeners how the message relates to them and how to apply the message is called *application*. If you want your message to change lives, include application information.

GUIDELINE #7: SPEAK FROM YOUR HEART

Present a message that matters to you—to people who matter to you. Let your listeners know that the subject is important to you and so are they. An effective preacher speaks not only to people's heads, but also to their hearts. He speaks to their hopes and dreams. He speaks to their discouragement, fears, and confusion.

Charles Spurgeon said, "Above all, he [the preacher] must put heart work into his preaching. He must feel what he preaches… I like the idea of pouring our sermons out of our own hearts. They must come from our hearts, or they will not go to our hearers' hearts."[2]

GUIDELINE #8: POINT OUT THAT THE BIBLE IS GOD'S LOVE LETTER TO HUMANS

Sometimes messages focus on correction and leave out the fact that God loves us and is trying to protect us with these teachings. God's love should permeate the message, even if it is a message of correction. It is the goodness of God that brings people to repentance (Romans 2:4).

GUIDELINE #9: KEEP IN MIND YOUR PURPOSE

In your audience, you will probably have a mixture of people. Some may not know anything about Jesus. Others may know a lot, but not be in relationship with Him. Some may be new Christians; others may be mature Christians.

Your job is to lead people to restoration and a right relationship with God. You are to help them step into repentance, salvation, baptism, maturation in Christ, edification, and equipping for service. We want messages that instruct, comfort, encourage, persuade, and inspire the listeners to take action. Don't just give them three interesting points and a poem.

GUIDELINE #10: INCLUDE A CALL FOR ACTION

What do you want your listeners to do? Encourage and challenge them to take action and do what you are recommending. Do you want them to pray and read the Bible every day? Do you want them to recognize their resentment and forgive themselves and others? Make it clear what your call to action is. And of course, an altar call is a call to action.

If you follow these guidelines, your listeners will understand how your message relates to them. They will be able to apply your teaching to their lives. And God's agenda will move forward through you.

CHAPTER 18

CHOOSE THE MESSAGE

The Bible is full of wonderful messages. It is the Word of God and the owner's manual for human beings. How do you choose which message to present? God has a plan. He knows who will be hearing your message. He knows what they need. He knows what He wants to do and how He wants to do it.

Your message choice is crucial. If you ran an auto supply store and a person came in needing a carburetor, it would not be helpful to say, "Here. I have a new steering wheel for you." If you ran a clothing store and a size 16 woman came in looking for a dress, it would not help her if you said, "Here is a beautiful size 10 dress."

Straight out of Bible school, a friend of mine preached to an elderly group on avoiding sexual sin. When I asked her how it went, she replied, "Well, I don't know. Maybe it was the wrong message for that group. They didn't seem very enthusiastic."

I once went to a series of meetings where most of the people were ministers and Bible school graduates. The focus was to equip the attendees to move up to the next level of their ministry calling. On the fifth night, the evangelist who was running the meetings surprised us all by preaching a salvation message. When he gave the call for salvation, a man who had not been to the other meetings came forward. Truly the Lord is the Good Shepherd who goes after the one lost sheep.

The evangelist later told us he was surprised when the Lord impressed on him the need to preach on salvation. He said it took self-discipline to put away his own thoughts regarding what would be the best message for our group.

HOW CAN YOU DISCOVER WHAT TO PREACH?

1. Pray for the right message. Ask God for the topic, Scriptures, and stories.

2. Read your Bible. The Holy Spirit may give you the topic or Scripture as you read the Word.

3. You may experience an intuitional knowing or inner urging to preach on a certain subject and Scripture. Follow your intuition.

4. Doug Jones, of Rhema Bible Training College, said that if you know what Bible-formed beliefs people need to embrace, then you know what to teach.[1] For example, what do people need to believe in order to be saved, baptized, or healed? What do they need to believe about tithing, kindness, or forgiveness?

5. Find out who will be in the audience. Match the message to the needs of the people. What are they struggling with? What are their fears? What frustrates them?

6. Current events can give you your topic. (After the terrorist attack on September 11, 2001, in the United States, people needed help dealing with the tragedy.)

7. Problems in the community can lead you to your topic (unemployment, poverty, crime).

8. Home and hospital visits may give you your topic. When you pray for people and counsel them, what topics or difficulties keep surfacing? Mark Sutton, pastor of Brookwood Baptist Church in Shreveport, Louisiana, comments, "... I began visiting in the homes of my members. I asked questions... They talked, I listened, and we all prayed... After these visits, I felt closer to my people. I knew better how to preach and teach so that needs were met."[2]

9. Seasonal messages may be God's choice (Christmas, Easter, Thanksgiving).

10. Your experiences may provide the topic. What has God helped you through? Depression? Bankruptcy? Alcoholism? Sickness? Fear? Abuse? Unbelief?

11. Don't assume you should speak about your latest revelation. Your listeners may be at a different spiritual level than you are. What is appropriate for you and your minister friends to discuss may not be the best teaching for the congregation.[3]

12. If you are a traveling minister and preach on the same topic each time, don't allow yourself to preach on automatic pilot. Make sure your message is fresh in your heart.

13. Give the listeners something to help them in their daily lives—something informational and inspirational. Preach positive, faith-filled, motivating messages.[4]

14. If the congregation is participating in a daily Bible-reading program (i.e., read through the Bible in a year), you might choose to preach on the current Scripture.

15. Pastors have the responsibility of feeding their congregation a Scripturally-balanced diet. If you are a pastor, you may want to plan your message themes ahead of time for the year, making sure to include the major doctrinal teachings. If you tumble from week to week in your planning, it is easy to omit an important area. Be ready to switch away from your planned theme if the Holy Spirit leads you in another direction.

16. Billy Joe Watts, of Rhema Bible Training College, suggested if you get stuck and cannot figure out what to preach, search your heart. What is God quickening in you? What moves you? There is something in your heart to share.[5]

17. You can preach through a book of the Bible in a series of messages, but be open for the Holy Spirit to redirect you and interrupt the series if He chooses.

18. If you are sick, tired, or heartbroken, and nothing appears to be the right topic, just feed your listeners the Word.[6] The Word is filled with power for those who believe it.

BIBLE LECTURES VS. BIBLE MESSAGES

In his book *Introducing the Sermon: The Art of Compelling Beginnings*, Michael J. Hostetler mentions that some preachers deliver Bible lectures and pass them off as sermons. Bible lectures are mainly educational. They seek to explain a Bible text. They tend not to be addressed to the needs of the audience. He states, "The sermon, on the other hand, is essentially motivational. It uses the explanation of the text as the basis for a personal or corporate response to God."[7]

KEEP YOUR GOAL IN MIND

As you write a message, keep your goal in mind. Don't just deliver a lecture. As a preacher, you are not a Bible professor speaking to Bible scholars. And you are not an after-dinner speaker aiming for lightweight entertainment. You have the responsibility of speaking for God, and He has a specific message for you to deliver each time you preach.

Make it your goal to deliver His message accurately and persuasively while you educate, encourage, correct, comfort, love, strengthen, and inspire His beloved people. The result will be salvation, healing, deliverance, joy, peace, and transformed lives. Wow! Isn't God wonderful?

CHAPTER 19

ORGANIZE THE MESSAGE PART I

Have you ever heard a preacher talk for five or ten minutes and not come to the point? Maybe you thought to yourself, *I wonder what he came to talk about. What could the subject be?*

One of our goals is to create an easily understandable message. What good is a message if it is so vague or scattered that the listeners don't understand it? We want to create clarity so that at the end of the message, the listener can say, "He talked about this. And he encouraged us to do this."

HOW TO ORGANIZE A MESSAGE

PRAYER

I read of a survey where pastors were asked, "How much time each day do you pray?" The answer surprised me. The average time spent in daily prayer was only five minutes.

When you organize a message, prayer is your first step. Pray for the main Scripture and all support Scriptures; the subject matter and main points; the stories, illustrations, and examples; and your opening and closing. God will help you organize.

PURPOSE

Identify the Purpose of the Message

When you step up to speak, it's important you know why you are going up there. In identifying your purpose, there are general and specific goals. What is your general goal? Public-speaking textbooks say there are three possible goals for a speech:

1. To educate/inform
2. To persuade/convince
3. To entertain

Secular speakers can choose one, two, or all three of these goals. But preachers don't have the luxury of choosing only the first or third. Preaching involves the first two goals and sometimes the third.

In his book *Handbook of Preaching*, Nathaniel M. Van Cleave states, "Preaching is the oral communication of divine truth with a view to persuasion. Preaching is not mere communication; it always has as a goal to motivate the hearers to make a decision and to take some form of action."[1]

We educate and inform, and sometimes we entertain with stories and examples. But our top general goal is to persuade. It is the one we dare not leave out.

We also have general goals that are specifically Christian: We want to help people get saved, healed, and delivered. We want to help people love and trust God.

Identify Your Specific Goal

Answer these questions.

1. What is your subject?
2. What is your main text (Scripture)?
3. What do you want your listeners to *know*?
4. What do you want your listeners to *do* when the message is over?
5. Is this message an answer to a need the listeners have? What is the need?

6. How can this message help people? What benefits will the listeners receive if they apply the message to their lives?

7. What is your bottom-line message? Write it in one sentence.

8. What is the title of your message?

You cannot convince your listeners of a truth if you don't know what it is you want them to know. You cannot persuade them to take action if you don't know what you want them to do. It is crucial that you identify the purpose of your message.

THE THREE PARTS OF A SPEECH

Any speech should have three parts. It will have an opening, a body, and a closing.

The OPENING

In the opening, you set the tone, momentum, and direction for the message. The goals of the opening are to:

- Gain the attention and interest of the listeners
- Establish rapport and connection
- Tell them what is to come
- Create positive expectation

Qualities of a Good Opening

Good openings have certain factors in common.

1. They are carefully prepared and have a well-thought-out opening sentence.
2. They are interesting.
3. They are confident—not apologetic.
4. They deal with one idea.

5. They are conversational—not highly emotional, impassioned, or loud.
6. They contain a clear statement of the theme and purpose of the message.
7. They show a benefit. They answer the listeners' questions: "What's in it for me?" and "Why is this message important?"
8. They are brief—only a minute or two.
9. They end with a transitional statement that links them to the body of the message.

What Is Included in an Opening?

Start with something interesting. It should relate to the main theme. It might be a question, story, anecdote, statistic, testimony, quotation, prop, or a statement of something you have in common with the listeners.

Mention the subject or title. For example: "Today we're going to talk about courage" or "Our title is: *How to Stand Strong When You're Afraid*."

Establish a need the message fills or the benefits that can result from applying the message.

Examples:

- "Have you ever wondered how to get your prayers answered?"
- "In this message, you will learn how to stop the works of the enemy by speaking the Words of God."
- "In this message, you will learn four ways to strengthen your home and family."
- "How many of you would like more peace of mind? If you apply today's message to your life, your peace of mind will increase."

Many preachers like to offer a prayer in the opening. If appropriate, read the main Scriptural text. End the opening with a transition that links the opening to the body.

Types of Openings

You can start your message in a variety of ways:

1. **Text** (main Scripture): In the textual opening, you announce the text. That is the main thrust of the opening. Some preachers simply say, "Our text for today is (John 3:16)." This opening is effective when most of the audience members understand that the Bible has answers for them.

2. **Context:** In the contextual opening, you discuss the context in which the Scriptural text exists.

    a. Give the background of the text.

    b. Summarize the meaning of surrounding Scriptures and what was going on in that chapter or book of the Bible.

    c. Mention the historical setting, political details, geography, customs, climate, place, and language nuances related to the text.

3. **Subject:** You can open by focusing on the subject. If the subject is "courage during difficult times," you might discuss the concept of courage and the benefits of developing it. Then launch into the text or an illustration.

    Example of a subject-related opening using the theme of humility: "Do you know any humble people? Are you humble? Scripture tells us that God gives grace to the humble. *Grace* means 'unmerited favor'—favor we don't deserve. Do you want God to give you grace? I do. I want God to give me grace, and I want Him to give you grace. Today we're going to talk about what it means to be humble. It used to be, in religious circles, that people thought being humble meant being poor. Financially poor. Broke. No money. But today, we're going to look in the Bible to find out what being humble means to God—so we can get in position to receive His favor."

4. **Title:** You might start by announcing the title. Billy Joe Daugherty, pastor at Victory Christian Center in Tulsa, Oklahoma, often opened with this statement: "The Word of the LORD is: (title of the message)." For instance, one Sunday he said, "The Word of the LORD is: God Will Perform His Word." He followed the title with a Scripture, story, anecdote, benefit, or explanatory statement, and then a transition into the body.

5. **Story or Anecdote:** In this opening, you start with an anecdote or story that relates to your theme. Many professional speakers begin this way. Their first words will be the beginning of the story. Reinhard Bonnke, the evangelist, opened a message with, "In the year 2,000, I was staying in a hotel in Lagos, and the LORD said to me…"

6. **The Objective:** When you open with the objective, you tell the listeners your goal. For an evangelistic message, you could open with: "Some of you don't have a personal relationship with God. I am going to present what God did for all humans through His Son, Jesus Christ, so that you may accept Him as your personal LORD and Savior. There's nothing more wonderful than stepping into the family of God."

    Here is another example: "How's your praise-meter? We know the Bible tells us to praise God, and many of us do when life is good. When things go our way and we're happy, it's easy to praise God. Thankful statements flow out of us like water out of a faucet. But what happens to our praise if we get laid off and have no job? No way to pay our bills. Or if we develop a serious illness or a family member dies? What happens to our praise when we face tough times? Today we're going to look at God's Word, and you will see that praising God in the middle of your difficulties will position you for protection."

7. **An Interesting or Startling Statement or Quotation:** In this opening, the speaker uses a startling statement to get people's

attention. If the title is, "Creating Strong Families," you might open with a statistic that claims there are more divorces among Christians than in the secular population.

8. **A Song Title, Verse, or Well-Known Saying from a Book, Movie, or Advertisement:** In this opening, you play off of some well-known words. I heard a preacher open with "How many of you remember the television series *Father Knows Best*?" He made a comment about the sitcom, then connected it to his title of "Father God Knows Best—His Rules Are Meant to Protect Us."

9. **Other Secular References:** You can use a newspaper article, sports story, quotation, or current event. When you open with a secular reference, make it relevant. Connect it to your theme.

10. **The Occasion:** The occasion may determine your opening. If you preach a funeral or a service following a national disaster, you may simply start with a prayer or a statement of purpose. For instance, "We are gathered here today to honor and celebrate the life of our dear friend, (name)." Or "We have come together today to find comfort and courage from the Word of God. The recent events…"

Write Out the Opening Word for Word

When you write it out, you will see wording that works. Craft the opening. Make it compact. Don't skip this step. Even for a personal story that you know well, write it down. Choose your opening sentence carefully. A missionary opened her message with, "It doesn't take a big person to carry the Word of God. It just takes a person."

Memorize the Opening

Don't read it. If you have to use notes, memorize at least the first minute. Your job is to connect with the audience in these first moments.

The BODY

The body of the speech will contain main ideas and support information. The body should include one to three main points. Never have more than five. Examples of support material for each main point are: Scriptures, quotations, statistics, stories, anecdotes, testimonies, illustrations, examples, explanation, and application.

Scriptures

For authoritative, persuasive preaching, show the listeners Scriptures that support the main points.

Quotations, Facts, Statistics, Stories, Anecdotes

Make sure these are interesting and directly relate to the point you are making.

Illustrations and Examples

Examples and illustrations explain and shed light on your message. You may use both positive and negative examples. For instance, if you teach on *Submission to God*, you could give examples of what it is, along with an example of what it is not.

Explanation

In the body, you will use different kinds of explanation. You may need to explain the main text or supporting Scriptures. You might explain the definition of words, the contextual meaning of the text, and bits of geographical, historical, or cultural background information. You also will need to explain doctrine.

When you talk about a specific character in the Bible, you may need to give a short summary of that person's story. Don't assume your listeners know the Bible stories.

Application

The most important part of a message is how it relates to the listener's life. Application includes:

- Answering the listener's questions. *(Why should I care about this message? What's in it for me? How is God trying to help me? How does God feel about me? What does God have for me? What does God want from me? What does God want me to do, think, or feel?)*

- Meeting the listeners' needs by addressing issues important to them.

- Showing the listeners how to apply the message to their lives.

- Giving altar calls that offer the listeners prayer for salvation, rededication to Christ, response to the theme of the message, or any other need.

At times, explanation and application will merge. John A. Broadus, in his classic book *On the Preparation and Delivery of Sermons* (4th edition with Vernon L. Stanfield), notes:

> Preaching ought to be not merely convincing and persuasive, but eminently instructive. The preacher often belabors men with arguments and appeals, when they are much more in need of practical and simple explanations of what to do and how to do it.[2]

No message is complete without application. If you omit this area, you have fallen short of your job. Weave application comments throughout the body; also mention them in the closing.

Simplicity

Keep the body simple and easy to follow. Don't give too much detailed information. Complex teachings may be interesting, but they are not easily remembered.

Use a transition when moving to each main point and before the closing.

The CLOSING

Your closing is your last chance to anchor the message in the listeners' minds and hearts and persuade them to take action. Craft your closing.

Qualities of a Good Closing

A good closing:

1. Is brief and to the point. It will not wander around with excess verbiage or vague generalities. In his book *How to Prepare Bible Messages*, James Braga notes that the closing should be so clear that the purpose of the message is obvious to the listeners.[3]

2. Wraps up the ideas to an ending point. There will be a sense of completion. The listeners will not be left feeling the discussion is unfinished.

3. Has a unity of focus. It will not be a scattershot of thoughts or introduce new ideas.

4. Is energetic. It will be sincere, earnest, or have godly zeal. It may be passionate, or emotional, or it may be quietly intense. It will never include trumped up or false emotions.

5. Seeks to persuade the listeners to apply the message to their lives. It will include a call for action, acceptance of a new thought, or a change of heart or attitude.

6. Speaks directly to the listeners. Address them as "you." Don't speak in abstractions, using "if *one* thinks" or "if *a person* thinks."

7. Encourages, comforts, guides, inspires, convinces, or challenges, but it does not scold.

8. Might use imagery to inspire the listeners. After discussing the children's mobile-street-ministry program, a speaker said, "*We need hands that are willing to go out and be God's heart extended.* You can make a difference in the life of a child. Come help us."

9. Often has a full-circle effect. You mention something in the closing that you spoke of in the opening. This creates a feeling of completeness and closure. You might repeat a question from the opening and answer it, or repeat the main Scripture, or make

reference to a story told in the opening. The previously mentioned missionary opened and closed with the same statement. After developing her plea for people to come out on the mission field, she closed by repeating her opening line, "It doesn't take a big person to carry the Word of God. It just takes a person." David used a full-circle effect in Psalm 8. He opened and closed with the same sentence: *"O Lord our Lord, how excellent is thy name in all the earth!"*

10. Ends when it is finished. It does not go on and on. It also does not end too soon before enough has been said to help listeners make a decision.

11. Flows in a natural way into the invitation and altar call.

What Is Included in a Closing?

You might choose to use a couple of these or many:

1. Summary or Review: Summarize the message, restate the proposition or objective, or repeat the leading thought.

2. Application: Tell the listeners how to use the message.

3. Illustration: Use a persuasive testimony.

4. Quotation: Use a famous person quote.

5. Repetition of the Scriptural Text

6. Appeal to Take Action

7. Prayer

8. Invitation or Altar Call

Write out the closing word for word and memorize it. Deliver it with eye contact and sincerity. Don't drop your energy level. Some speakers have an effective opening and body but fizzle out at the end. The closing is your last moment to influence your audience. Keep it focused and energetic.

TRANSITIONS

A transition creates a bridge between what you just talked about and what you are going to talk about next. It tells the listeners you are moving on to the next idea. A transition should come after the opening and after each main point.

Transitional Sentences

Transitional sentences are very effective because they can explain where you have been and where you are headed.

Examples of transitional sentences:

1. "Now that we have looked at *why* we praise God, let's look at *how* we praise God."

2. "We have seen in these Scriptures that one way God heals is through the laying on of hands. Now let's look at another way God heals people."

I like summary-type transitional sentences. They clarify the meaning and help corral the listeners' wandering thoughts. Write them ahead of time. Don't assume you can think them up while you preach.

Other Types of Transitions

You can use transitional words or phrases.

1. "first, second, third" or "number one, number two, number three"

2. "now, furthermore, therefore, lastly, also"

3. "now then," "let's look at," "and consider this," "on the other hand," "in addition to"

Sometimes questions make good transitions.

1. "But what about Paul's thorn in the flesh?"

2. "What else will help us forgive when we don't want to?"

3. "What is another characteristic of God's nature?"

Transition Between the Announcements and the Message

If you are doing both the announcements and the message, you need a transition between the two. You can use a transitional pause—a long moment of quiet. Or you can use a shift in body position; a change of tone, vocal pacing, or volume; a statement; or a prayer to signal the beginning of the message. You can also have the listeners change position. For instance, after making the announcements, you could say, "Let's all stand." Then you pray the opening prayer.

Key Point: If you use transitions after the opening and after the main points, your message will be easier to follow.

CHAPTER 20

ORGANIZE THE MESSAGE PART II

When I took a speech class in college, my professor refused to give me an "A," even though he told me I was an excellent speaker. He only gave me a "B" grade because I did not know how to outline my speeches. I have since found outlining to be a mainstay for speech and message writing.

I encourage you to create an outline for every message you preach. Outlining will help you see if you are organized and focused and if you have enough support material.

HOW TO CREATE AN OUTLINE

The Heading

At the top of your outline page, put the following headings. Fill them out as soon as possible.

Subject:

Title:

Text: (main Scripture)

Summary Statement: (The essence of the message in one sentence.)

Objective: (The desired action or result of the message.)

Benefit(s): (If the listeners use this message, how will they benefit?)

Example:

Subject: Praise

Title: The Power of Praise

Text: Acts 16:25–26

Summary Statement: Praising God positions us for Divine protection.

Objective: The listeners will see the power in praise, and they will increase their praise in their daily lives.

Benefit: They will be in position for more of God's protection in their lives.

I cannot emphasize strongly enough that it is important to know the summary statement and objective of your message.

EXAMPLE OF AN OUTLINE

The Three Parts of a Message

I. The OPENING will include some of the following:

  A. Something interesting to get people's attention that relates to the main theme

      1. A question

      2. A story or anecdote

      3. An interesting statistic or fact

      4. A testimony

      5. A quotation

      6. A prop

      7. A statement of what you have in common with the audience or something about them or their town

8. The need that the message addresses
9. Secular references that relate to the theme
10. An unusual or startling statement
11. A song title, verse, or well-known saying

B. Subject and/or title
C. Benefits that can result from applying the message
D. Prayer
E. Main Scriptural text (if appropriate at that time)
F. Context of the Bible text
   1. The story line of the chapter or book of the Bible you are using
   2. The meaning of surrounding verses
   3. Politics, geography, customs, historical references, climate, place, language nuances
G. The summary statement and/or objective
H. Special occasion comments
I. A transition

II. The BODY will include some of these elements:

A. One to three main points (never more than five)
B. Support material for each point
   1. Scriptures
   2. Quotations
   3. Facts and interesting statistics
   4. Stories and anecdotes
   5. Testimonies

      6. Illustrations and examples

      7. Explanation

      8. Application

          a. Show how and why the message relates to the listeners' lives

          b. Tell the benefits of applying the message

          c. Tell how to apply the message to their lives

  C. A transition after each main point

III. The CLOSING may include:

  A. Summary or review

      1. Summarize the message

      2. Review the main points

      3. Repeat the leading thought of the message

  B. Application

      1. Tell how to apply the message to their lives

      2. Repeat-after-me prayers

      3. Altar call

  C. Call to action

      1. Encourage the listeners to do what you are recommending

      2. Predict their success when they do it

  D. Inspirational ending that ties into the opening

  E. Prayer

  F. Altar call or invitation for these areas:

      1. Salvation

      2. Recommitment to Christ

3. Prayer related to the message theme
4. Prayer for any other reason

Note: In an outline, information is indented under its category.

HOW TO SHORTEN OR LENGTHEN THE MESSAGE

In your outline, plan how to shorten or lengthen your message. If you are scheduled to speak for thirty minutes but the program is overtime, the meeting planner might only give you fifteen. Or the reverse might happen. You may be ready to speak for twenty minutes but find out you have sixty. You should already know how you will shorten or expand the message.

Three Ways to Shorten or Lengthen a Message

1. **Keep the same main points but add or delete support material.**
   You can add or delete Scriptures, stories, illustrations, testimonies, etc. under the main points. So you stretch out the message, or you shrink it. The basic message stays the same. This is the easiest approach. I put extra support Scriptures, stories, or illustrations in my outline so I know how to expand the message if necessary. But I put a star beside the most important ones so I am sure to use them if I am short of time. One of the benefits of this approach is that your summary, during the closing, does not change.

2. **Add or delete main points and their support material.**
   In this approach, you delete or add a whole section—the main point and its support material. Since summaries of main points are often included in the closing, you need to adapt the closing to reflect the changes.

3. **Add or delete audience participation activities.**

Note: Speakers often speak faster than normal when they are nervous. You may need the lengthier version.

THE SURE-FIRE SUCCESS FORMULA

This well-known technique is often used by professional speakers and preachers. It helps the listener mentally organize the message. This formula uses the three parts of a speech—opening, body, and closing. It is also called the *Three Ts "Tell Them" Approach*.

1. In the opening: Tell them what you are going to tell them.
(You mention what you are going to talk about.)
2. In the body: Tell them. (You go ahead and talk about it.)
3. In the closing: Tell them what you told them.
(You review and summarize the main points.)

The clarity of this organizational pattern can set you up for success.

HOLY SPIRIT-LED PREPARATION

God's speakers need to be Holy Spirit-led in their preparation as well as in their presentation.

Some speakers believe they don't need to prepare. I have seen preachers (who did no preparation) stand at the lectern with nothing to say. They expected the Holy Spirit to fill their mouth with words, but it did not happen.

A friend of mine went on a missions trip to India. She knew she would be talking to a group of 350 Christian women. When she returned home, I asked her how it went. She said, "I wish I had prepared something."

Some preachers don't prepare in the way I am recommending. But they do pray and mull over a Scripture (and its theme). God gives some people the ability to preach effectively with that kind of preparation or even none. If that is you, that's fine. I am not saying there is only one way to prepare (or preach). But if you are a spur-of-the-moment preacher, I hope you will look through the preparation suggestions and choose the ones that can strengthen your preaching.

When you step up to the lectern, if the Holy Spirit says to abandon your prepared message and preach a different one, then step out in faith and follow His lead.

CHAPTER 21

CHOOSE THE RIGHT WORDS: GENERAL GUIDELINES

One of the temptations that comes with attending a seminary or Bible school is that you may learn big theological words and want to use them. I remember listening to a talented seminary student preach. In his opening sentence, he used a theological term I had never heard. Throughout his message, my brain kept saying to me, *What does that word mean?* Even though I knew I was yielding to distraction, I could not let the word go to focus 100% on his message.

Does it matter what kind of words you use when you preach? Are there word choices that will increase the likelihood that listeners will understand and remember your message? Are there expressions you should avoid? Yes, yes, and yes.

SIMPLICITY

I have heard preachers present messages in which they analyzed Greek words in painstaking detail. If the audience had been seminary students, it would have been fine. But we were just a normal congregation looking for help in our daily lives. Some of the listeners may have gone away thinking, "We sure have a smart preacher." But did he connect with them? No. Did he give them something that helped them? No. Did he persuade them to take action in any of God's ways? No.

Use basic, everyday words. Don't show off your large vocabulary or try to awe people with your knowledge of theology. Keep your words simple.

SENTENCE LENGTH

Occasionally I hear speakers who wander around in long, convoluted sentences. Sometimes I have thought, *What did he say? That did not make any sense.* Short sentences create clarity. For the sake of variety, every now and then put in a long sentence, but most of the time use short sentences.

ABBREVIATIONS

Don't use an abbreviation for a word unless you explain it (i.e., "I was a PK—a preacher's kid"). Otherwise, people who don't know the meaning may feel like they don't belong. This can separate you from the very people you want to connect with.

JARGON

Every group has specific in-group language. Explain the Christian sayings you use. Your listeners want to know what you are talking about. For instance, if you encourage people to witness for Christ, don't just say, "Preach Christ and Him crucified!" Explain what that means. Give them an example of words they could say.

If you use words like *unction, works, born again, the flesh, the blood,* or *dying to self,* tell what they mean. If you say, "Keep your eyes on Jesus," or "Be fruitful," tell them how to do it. Even the term *believer* can be confusing because everyone believes in something. Sometimes God's message is not received because the preacher speaks "Christianese," and the listener does not know that language.

SLANG

Slang is informal speech that coins new words or changes the meaning of others. In the youth culture, each new generation creates its own meaning for certain words, such as: *cool, radical, boss, hot, bad,* or *sweet.* Youth pastors and inner-city ministers often use slang effectively. Be aware of your slang expressions. Do your listeners understand them? The important thing is to make your word choices appropriate to your audience.

SARCASM

Webster's New World Dictionary defines *sarcasm* as "a taunting or caustic remark, generally ironic." *Ironic* is defined as "meaning the contrary of what is expressed."[1]

Sarcasm can convey veiled anger, resentment, or annoyance. You may get laughter from it, but it may be at someone's expense. Some listeners feel unsafe and will shut down emotionally in the presence of sarcasm. It may cause them to distrust you and feel uncared about.

If you make sarcastic comments, ask yourself these questions:

- Am I making fun of someone?
- Am I ridiculing or criticizing a person or a group of people?
- Am I venting my frustration?
- Am I expressing impatience or annoyance at a person, group of people, or situation?

If the audience becomes quiet and unresponsive and the minister says, "Thank you for your enthusiasm. I love your encouragement" or "Don't all amen me at once," he has used sarcasm.

The keys to whether such statements work in a positive way are attitude, tone of voice, and personality. I have seen good-natured preachers make these statements, and the people knew they were not being criticized. But other preachers (using the same statements) sounded bitter because they were annoyed at the listeners.

INSULTS

Once I observed a speaker tease the audience members about their accent. He was attempting to connect, but his words insulted some of them and created an adversarial relationship.

Some preachers criticize other Christian denominations from the pulpit. Creating dissension among brothers is not good. If we disrespect each other, how can we expect people to want to join us?

HUMOR

Humor relaxes people and helps concentration, attention, and memory. But be careful what kind of humor you use. Jokes are not the best choice for humor from the pulpit. They are risky. What is funny to you may be offensive to someone else. If you are determined to use a joke, make sure it is not morbid, sexual, racial, ethnic, bathroom-themed, or gender-based (male vs. female). Also, it should relate to your theme.

How can you add humor without telling jokes? Use anecdotes. If they turn out funny, they add a fun dimension. But if not, they still offer a helpful analogy, and you have not just used a joke that fell flat on its face.

Another way to add humor is to toss in a light-hearted comment. When Billy Joe Daugherty used the word *acquiesce* in a message, he realized he had used a word some people might not know. He corrected the situation by saying, "*Acquiesce* means 'to give in.'" Then he paused and said, "I know a few big words—*acquiesce* and *mayonnaise*."[2]

Another preacher, while teaching on prayer, encouraged the congregation to pray in different situations. He said, "You can pray while you drive." He paused and then added, "Just don't close your eyes."

CULTURAL SAYINGS AND IDIOMS

Every culture has its own unusual expressions that don't mean what the words say. People from different cultures listen to you. Idioms can confuse them. Examples: *That takes the cake! He took a leap in the dark. She's got too much on her plate. It's not my cup of tea. Let's throw in the towel.* If you use an idiom, explain it. For instance, you might say: "I've got bigger fish to fry—I've got more important things to do." Be aware of the idioms you use. Eliminate them or explain them.

DEFINITIONS AND EXPLANATIONS

Many people don't understand the basic words in the Bible. It helps if you explain them. Some preachers laboriously quote dictionary definitions. Don't do that. You can define and explain without becoming tedious. One of my pastors used Psalm 103 as the text for a message on "God Is Good." He read the first verse (*"Bless the* Lord, *O my soul: and all that is within me, bless his holy name"*). Then he explained, "*Bless* means 'to rejoice, magnify, praise, and give thanks' to the Lord. Your *soul* is your mind, emotions, and will." He communicated the meaning in only eight seconds.

THE DISCRETIONARY RULE FOR WHAT *NOT* TO INCLUDE IN YOUR MESSAGE

My grandfather used to say, "If in doubt, don't." This rule can simplify your decision-making. Do you have a story about your kids, and you're wondering whether to tell it? If you think maybe you shouldn't, then don't.

Do you have a joke to illustrate a point that has a tinge of sexism or dark humor? Maybe you think to yourself, *Well it's not quite right, but it's funny. It'll lighten things up.* Should you use it? No.

Perhaps you know a story about someone that would make a great illustration. But you don't have the person's permission to use it, and you notice you are asking yourself, "Is this okay?" *If in doubt, don't.*

If you have a hesitation about including something in your message, God may be leading you through your intuition. *If in doubt, don't.*

PREJUDICE AND OFFENSIVE LABELS

I read an article about Mahatma Gandhi, the leader of the nonviolent Indian independence movement. He was quoted as saying that he thought Christ could have been the answer for India, but the prejudicial treatment he received from Christians made Christ an impossible choice for him and his countrymen.

A friend of mine, who is of Native American descent, visited a church hoping to find a place of belonging. During the message, the pastor made disparaging remarks about Native Americans. After the message, my friend told the pastor she had been hurt by his comments and would not be returning.

Humans have prejudice. God does not. He values all people equally. Are you representing Him accurately? Preachers have a responsibility to rid themselves of prejudice.

> *Though I speak with the tongues of men and of angels, and have not charity* [love], *I am become as sounding brass, or a tinkling cymbal. And though I have the gift of prophecy, and understand all mysteries, and all knowledge; and though I have all faith, so that I could remove mountains, and have not charity* [love], *I am nothing.* (1 Corinthians 13:1–2)

THE SANCTITY OF THE PULPIT

Some preachers use the pulpit for personal tirades. They vent their negative emotions, displaying frustration, anger, and bitterness. Don't misuse or abuse your authority. If you cannot resolve your personal frustrations, lay them aside while you preach. Speaking for God is a sacred honor. We need to preserve the sanctity of the pulpit and represent Him correctly.

CHAPTER 22

USE IMAGERY TO ANCHOR A CONCEPT

One night as I cleared dishes off my dining room table, T.D. Jakes, pastor of The Potter's House in Dallas, Texas, was preaching on television. His voice drifted across the room saying, "Sometimes Christians lose their fire. They dry up on the inside. They don't want to pray anymore or read their Bible. *They get all dried up like a piece of old toast left on the counter overnight.*" I stopped in my tracks, halfway to the sink. His imagery immobilized me. I could see the dried up, stiff piece of toast in my mind's eye. I still remember his message because of the picture he painted with his words.

The Bible is an imagery-rich book. It is filled with mental pictures created by stories, parables, testimonies, metaphors, similes, analogies, illustrations, and concrete examples. Jesus used all these. The Psalms, Proverbs, and Song of Solomon are saturated with imagery. They bring to mind one picture after another, enabling us to grab a concept through association with something we are familiar with.

The use of imagery—the ability to create pictures in the listener's mind—is a skill all preachers need to develop.

Benefits of Using Imagery

1. Imagery gets and holds a person's attention.
2. Imagery sheds light on and illustrates an idea.
3. Imagery helps explain a situation or concept.

4. Imagery helps people remember.
5. Imagery creates interest and fun for the listener.
6. Imagery keeps your message from being dry or boring.

METAPHORS, SIMILES, AND OTHER ANALOGIES

The Bible is filled with the word-picture techniques known as metaphors, similes, and analogies. They teach us what to do and what not to do. They help us understand who God is, how He helps us, and who we are to Him. They create pictures that stay in our minds so we remember God's truth.

Metaphor

A metaphor is a figure of speech in which one thing is spoken of as if it were another. Examples: Jesus *is* our Rock. He *is* the door, the way, the Light. God *is* our refuge. "*I **am** the vine, ye **are** the branches*" (John 15:5).

When Jacob was on his deathbed, he spoke about each of his sons. In Genesis 49, he used metaphors when he said, "*Judah **is** a lion's whelp… Issachar **is** a strong donkey… Naphtali **is** a deer let loose… Joseph **is** a fruitful bough… Benjamin **is** a ravenous wolf…*"

The book of Proverbs gives us wonderful examples of metaphors:

- "*Wine **is** a mocker*" (Proverbs 20:1a).
- "*The fear of the* L<small>ORD</small> ***is** a fountain of life*" (Proverbs 14:27a).
- "*A wholesome tongue **is** a tree of life*" (Proverbs 15:4a).

John Hagee, pastor of Cornerstone Church in San Antonio, Texas, used the following metaphor: "Forgiveness *is* the key that unlocks the handcuffs of resentment." A friend of mine went to a Bible-study group where the speaker talked about the *vultures* that attack a new vision. The vultures were things like doubt, fear, laziness, and distractions. The word *vulture* gives us an immediate negative image. Think how bland the Bible-study lesson would have been if the topic had been the *situations* or *things* that attack a new vision.

Simile

The simile compares one thing with another by saying it is *like* the object mentioned. It uses the words: *like, as,* or *as if.*

Scriptural examples of similes:

1. "*The words of a talebearer are **as** wounds*" (Proverbs 18:8a).

2. "*Then did I beat them small **as** the dust before the wind*" (Psalm 18:42a).

3. "*A merry heart doeth good **like** a medicine*" (Proverbs 17:22a).

In a series of messages on bitterness, Billy Joe Daugherty used these similes:

- Holding on to bitterness is *like strapping a dead body to your body.*

- Resentment is *like drinking poison and expecting your enemy to die.*

- Getting offended is *like going to the airport with too much baggage.*[1]

A Christian education director, who spoke about timidity in witnessing, said, "Fear, *like a muzzle on a dog,* keeps me silent, and I say nothing." In her book, *What the Bible Is All About,* Henrietta C. Mears states, "Persecution almost always has spread the gospel *like wind spreads fire.*"[2]

Sometimes it helps to explain the simile. John C. Maxwell said, "Life is a lot *like tennis*—the one who can serve best seldom loses."[3]

Imagery Using Nature or Animals

Is your message about surviving after a defeat? Notice a redwood tree—majestic and tall even though a fire has burned out part of the trunk.

The Holy Spirit uses our knowledge of animals to make a point.

- "*For ye were as sheep going astray*" (1 Peter 2:25).

- "*Go to the ant, thou sluggard; consider her ways, and be wise*" (Proverbs 6:6).

Think of the physical and personality characteristics of different animals. If you are trying to motivate people to deal with a problem they are ignoring, you could say: "You think it's a cute little kitten? No. It's a sleeping tiger in your house. The question is, will you recognize it and deal with it before it wakes up?"

Imagery from nature has a universal appeal. It is not limited to one country or culture.

Vary Your Analogies

Your analogies will appeal to more people if you will vary the type. Analogies can be created using almost any category.

- Sports Analogies: "Run the race of life." "Be a team member. Grab the baton and do your part." "Step up to the plate; God has work for you to do."

- Cooking Analogies: "God has given us a recipe for success. Let's look at the ingredients." "Too many cooks spoil the stew. You need to be in a church under the guidance of one pastor—not bouncing around from church to church."

- Gardening and Farming Analogies: "Be good soil." "Bloom where you're planted." "Sow a seed of kindness."

- Weather Analogies: "When you go through a dry spell" "The storms of life"

- Math Analogies: "Here is the bottom line." "What you told me doesn't add up."

- Art Analogies: "God, like a potter shaping the clay on the wheel of life" "Weave your life like a tapestry. Make it interesting."

- Animal Analogies: "Let's get our ducks lined up in a row." "This project is moving at a snail's pace."

- Nature Analogies: "When you're on the mountain top" "Walking through the valley"

ANECDOTES

The use of anecdotes is the most valuable tool I learned as a speaker. This technique can make you an interesting and even riveting speaker—someone people love listening to. An anecdote is a short, interesting account of something that really happened. Anecdotes are terrific at creating connection with your listeners. When you use a personal story, you invite them into your life. And they feel like you trust them and are their friend.

You can enliven your messages by turning daily experiences into anecdotes that relate to your theme. In order to do this, you need to remember them. How can you do that?

How to Remember Anecdotes

Write down ten experiences from your life. Don't write out each story yet. First write down a phrase that is a title for each one.

Examples:

1. The day I got trampled
2. I broke the pastor's rule
3. Waking up in a foul mood

Tap Into Your Memory Bank

To stimulate your memory, it helps to think of categories of memories.[4] To do this, we can use the word P-R-E-A-C-H-I-N-G as an acrostic.

Parents: What happened when you stole a package of gum? What was important to your father? What advice did your parents give you?

Recreation: What made your canoe overturn? How did you learn to swim? What was your best vacation?

Education: Who was your favorite teacher and why? Why did a professor yell at you? What helped you pass a chemistry test?

<u>A</u>nimals: Have you had pets? Which one was your favorite? Why? Have you ever had a dangerous experience with an animal?

<u>C</u>hores: What chores did you love or hate? What was your first job for pay?

<u>H</u>elpers: Which people helped you at different stages in your life? Who influenced you the most? Who encouraged you?

<u>I</u>nterests: How do you enrich the soil for a garden? What meal are you good at cooking? What is your favorite free-time activity?

<u>N</u>ature: Do you remember an incident involving snakes or hornets? What experiences do you have with oceans, rivers, or lakes? What did you do during a tornado, earthquake, or flood? Have you ever fought a fire?

<u>G</u>roceries: What happened when you pulled out thirty coupons and ten people were in line behind you? What did you do when you were given back too much change?

Pay attention in your daily life. Your days are filled with seemingly insignificant occurrences. You can turn them into interesting anecdotes.

Identify the Idea

After you have ten titles, think about what you learned from each experience. What point could you make while using each story? Find a concept the story illustrates. Write it down next to each story title.

Examples:

1. The day I got trampled: God is in the protection business.
2. I broke the pastor's rule: Obedience to God's line of authority is important.

3. Waking up in a foul mood: Praising God can break the power of oppression.

Now that you have identified life experiences and the concepts they illustrate, choose one that fits your message. Write the story down. Use specific and compact wording. Include details but not unnecessary ones. Write an explanatory sentence telling the connection between the story and your theme.

Keep adding to your list of experiences. Store them with title and concept in an anecdote/stories file.

Common Mistakes When Using Anecdotes

Some speakers make the mistake of not writing down the anecdote or rehearsing it. When you write it, you will discover ways to use powerful wording, condense the story, and incorporate interesting story-telling techniques (i.e., dialogue, body movement, etc.). Without rehearsal, you may weaken the story with too many words and use up precious time.

Another common mistake is that the speaker fails to identify a concept from the anecdote that relates to the theme. Clearly communicate the connection between the anecdote and your message.

Note: It's okay to tell a cute, unrelated anecdote about your children, pets, etc., but tell your listeners it is not related to your theme.

TESTIMONIES

A testimony is a personal story of how God helped a certain person in a specific situation.

Throughout the Bible, we are told to speak of God's wonderful works and His goodness. Testimonies do that. They increase faith, build hope, and produce expectation. They help the listeners believe God is good and His Word is true.

In Acts 26, the apostle Paul uses his own testimony as he attempts to persuade King Agrippa. He mentions his history of persecuting Christians and then of his Damascus road experience. In Acts 11:1–18, Peter speaks his testimony. He explains what influenced him to break Jewish rules of conduct and preach the message of Jesus to Cornelius and his family.

You may include your own testimony, or you might have someone come up and tell theirs. Ask people ahead of time if they are willing to share their testimony. I heard a minister say from the pulpit, "Oh, So and So, why don't you stand up and tell the people your wonderful testimony of how Jesus delivered you from multiple immoral relationships?" The woman the minister addressed slumped her shoulders, lowered her head, and stared at the ground.

If you tell someone else's testimony, get written permission first. One of the most common errors made by speakers is ignoring the boundaries of privacy and confidentiality. No matter how riveting the testimony, remember that confidentiality is part of your job. If you tell a story someone told you in confidence, your disclosure may harm that person or their family.

"The words of a talebearer are as wounds, and they go down into the innermost parts of the belly" (Proverbs 18:8). Keep private things private—unless you have the person's permission or unless it is your own story and the Holy Spirit gave you the go-ahead to tell it.

Why have I separated stories and testimonies? A testimony will give evidence and proof of the goodness of God, and it will give glory to Him. A story might only have a helpful concept in it.

STORIES

Large amounts of the Bible are written in narrative story form. The creation story, the fall of man, the choosing of Abraham, the birth of Jesus, His life and works, the acts of the apostles—they are all stories.

Why does the Holy Spirit teach us with stories? Because people love stories. They hold our attention and help us learn and remember.

Stories can be from your life, other people's lives, history, the Bible, magazines, etc. They are a great teaching tool, but keep them short.

Note: Don't ever make up stories and pretend they are real. And don't ever use someone else's story and pretend it happened to you.

GENERALIZED PERSONAL EXPERIENCES

You can create a summarized, general remark from the lives of several people. You could say something like, "Many of the people I have talked to over the years have struggled with _____. They often say _____. They may feel that _____. And they think that _____. Some of you may be in the same situation. I have good news for you. God is here to help you. Let's open our Bibles and see what God says about this situation."

Example: "Many of the people I have talked to over the years have struggled with depression. They often say that life doesn't seem to matter anymore. They may feel that they are helpless. And they think that it is hopeless and God is far from them. Some of you may be in the same situation. I have good news for you. God is here to help you. Let's open our Bibles and see what God says about depression."

DIALOGUE

The Bible uses dialogue frequently. In the midst of a narrative, dialogue is inserted. Reading Genesis 4, *"Am I my brother's keeper?"* is a vibrant experience. Without dialogue, think how dull it would be to read: *Cain asked the Lord if he was his brother's keeper.* Using dialogue in a story or anecdote adds a fresh touch. It livens things up.

Examples of how to change a statement into dialogue format:

1. Instead of saying, "He told me not to go," say, "He said, *'Don't go!'*"

2. Instead of saying, "She asked me why I did that," say, "She asked, *'Why did you do that?'*"

3. Instead of saying, "You might be wondering why I think that," say, "You might be saying to yourself, *'Why does he think that?'*"

When you speak dialogue, use vocal variety. Vary your tone, pitch, volume, or inflectional pattern.

ILLUSTRATIONS

When you use illustrations, you choose something the listeners have knowledge about in daily life to explain an idea or principle.

Consider this illustration: In a dry state like California, a spark from a campfire or cigarette can start a forest fire that races across hundreds of acres destroying everything in its path. The book of James says the tongue is a fire. Just like a spark, careless words can create a path of destruction.

Joel Osteen, pastor of Lakewood Church in Houston, Texas, used this illustration: "If you owned an apartment building and rented out 80% of the apartments to drug dealers and thieves, pretty soon they would have run off the 20% good people. In the same way, you rent out space in your brain to your thoughts. Don't spend most of your time thinking about your problems. Don't dwell on depressive thoughts. Rent out space to good thoughts."[5]

In her book *Celebration of Simplicity*, Joyce Meyer said: "It is important to forgive quickly. The quicker we do it, the easier it becomes. A weed that has deep roots is harder to pull out than one that has just sprung up."[6]

STATEMENT OF HUMAN BEHAVIOR

You can use a statement of human behavior to create an illustration.

- "Consider the person who _____." Example: "*Consider the person who* is cordial, polite, and even kind to people at the office, but when he gets home he throws temper tantrums—yelling at his wife and children."

- "Let's say you find yourself in this position: you _____." Example: *"Let's say you find yourself in this position: you* want to be a loyal worker and a loving Christian at the office, but your boss belittles you and scolds you in front of clients."

- "What if _____?" Example: "*What if* you want to forgive a person who damaged you, but you can't? What should you do?"

EXAMPLES

Some people don't apply a teaching to themselves unless you mention their specific situation. In Ephesians 5:21–6:9, Paul teaches about how people should treat each other. He uses the examples of wives, husbands, children, fathers, servants, and masters.

When preaching on "God Is Bigger than Your Problem," Bruce Edwards, associate pastor of Victory Christian Center in Tulsa, Oklahoma, mentioned many different problems. He said something like this: "God is bigger than your problem. He is bigger than cancer. He is bigger than divorce. He is bigger than depression, pornography, or unemployment. No matter what your problem, God wants to pour out His power, love, and mercy upon you."

If you preach on the importance of developing self-discipline, you could ask:

"What is it you don't like to do? Mow the lawn? Scour the toilet? Clean the cat box? Balance the checkbook? What in your life takes self-discipline? How about reading your Bible or praying? What important thing in your life will not get done without self-discipline?"

If you use a variety of examples, you will help your listeners connect with your message.

IMAGERY RELATED TO THE LISTENERS' LIFESTYLE

Think about common experiences your listeners encounter. If you refer to situations they are familiar with, you increase your ability to reach them. Jesus showed how to do this.

- In Jesus' time, people lived in an agricultural society. So He used agricultural imagery. *"Behold, a sower went forth to sow"* (Matthew 13:3b).

- Most people have had the experience of getting a foreign object in their eye. *"And why beholdest thou the mote that is in thy brother's eye, but perceivest not the beam that is in thine own eye?"* (Luke 6:41).

- Building houses was a common occurrence. *"He is like a man which built an house, and digged deep, and laid the foundation on a rock"* (Luke 6:48a).

- Lending and owing money was part of the culture. "*There was a certain creditor which had two debtors: the one owed five hundred pence, and the other fifty*" (Luke 7:41).

I heard a preacher talk about the "GPS" (Global Positioning System) in cars. It tells the driver how to get to a certain destination. He said the Bible is our "GPS." It is "God's Positioning System." If you speak to a group of young single people, you won't use illustrations about raising children. If you preach to people who live in a wilderness setting, you won't tell your lawn-mowing stories.

Throughout the Bible, God gives us one example after another of how to communicate with imagery. Using imagery is not a luxury. It is a necessity.

CHAPTER 23

CREATE MEMORABLE WORDING

In his 1961 inaugural address, John F. Kennedy (the 35th president of the United States), made this comment: "And so, my fellow Americans: ask not what your country can do for you—ask what you can do for your country." These words ignited a sense of hope that we could work together to make our country a better place. They inspired people to pull together in a team effort. We anticipated a great future.

What makes an inspirational statement? The above quote contains careful word-crafting. The following ways to create memorable wording are tools of the speaking trade. They increase the listener's memory and enjoyment of the message. Think of speakers who inspire you. You will recognize their use of these techniques. These tools can transform an ordinary statement into an inspiring quotation.

ALLITERATION

My mother loved alliteration. When a small road was put next to our loquat tree, she named the road *Loquat Lane*. Alliteration uses words that start with the same first sound.

1. "Tithing of Time, Talent, and Treasure"

2. "Prayer That Ushers in the Power and Presence of God"

3. *"who <u>w</u>alketh upon the <u>w</u>ings of the <u>w</u>ind"* (Psalm 104:3c)

4. *"the clouds <u>d</u>rop <u>d</u>own the <u>d</u>ew"* (Proverbs 3:20)

Alliteration can be fun, but use it sparingly. Overuse can trivialize your message.

REPETITION

People have many thoughts in their minds. Their focus may move in and out on what you are saying. Repetition helps the brain remember. Emphasize important points by repeating them. You can repeat the sentence you just spoke (i.e., "God knew you before the foundation of the earth. God knew *you* before the foundation of the earth!")

You can repeat the main idea. In a message on the love of God, you can keep repeating, "God loves you!" Martin Luther King Jr., the American civil rights leader, used repetition in his classic, "I Have a Dream," speech. He kept repeating, "I have a dream!"

Psalm 107 repeats the plea of the Holy Spirit four times: *"Oh that men would praise the LORD for his goodness, and for his wonderful works to the children of men!"* Psalm 136 uses repetition twenty-six times with the phrase, *"for his mercy endureth for ever."* Anything we hear over and over again becomes a part of us. You can use repetition to plant good thoughts in your listeners' minds.

You can repeat a group of words to create a rhythm. Paul did this in 2 Timothy 4:7: *"I have fought a good fight, I have finished my course, I have kept the faith."* A preacher might say, "Don't be afraid—God is for you! Don't be afraid—God is with you! Don't be afraid—God is in you!" You might hear rhythmic repetition in a call to action: "Choose life—choose to repent! Choose life—choose to forgive! Choose life—choose to love!"

RULE OF THREE

Three words, three phrases, or three sentences together create a pleasing rhythm and something powerful I cannot explain. They are a tool of eloquence that can carry your message into people's hearts and minds.

Examples of the Rule of Three

1. I heard a pastor open his message with this question: "Are you tired, broke, and worn-out?"

2. In *The Purpose Driven Life*, Rick Warren wrote, "Love should be your top priority, primary objective, and greatest ambition."[1]

3. In 2 Timothy 4:7, Paul said, *"I have fought a good fight, I have finished my course, I have kept the faith."*

PARALLEL STRUCTURE

Parallel structure creates a balance by using a repetition of some grammatical element. The similarity may be a repetition of a part of speech such as a verb tense, a repetition of sentence structure, or a repeated use of some other part of the sentence. When our sentences sound choppy and awkward, sometimes the problem is due to faulty parallelism.

In her book *Grammatically Correct*, Anne Stilman says that if you use parallelism in a sentence, list, or group of items, you will not jump from the active voice to the passive, from the second person to the third, from the present tense to the past, or from a series of verbs to a noun.[2]

Examples of Parallel Structure

1. "God is holy. God is pure. And God is good." "God is _____" is repeated. The blank is filled in with an adjective. These sentences would not be parallel if they said, "God is holy. God is my fortress. And God is always wanting to help you." The element that makes the wording parallel is the repeated use of an adjective in the blank.

2. "<u>I have fought</u> a good fight, <u>I have finished</u> my course, <u>I have kept</u> the faith" (2 Timothy 4:7). Paul repeated the use of *I* plus the past participle verb form. The repetition of the verb form makes it parallel.

3. "And he leaping up <u>stood</u>, and <u>walked</u>, and <u>entered</u> with them into the temple, <u>walking</u>, and <u>leaping</u>, and <u>praising</u> God" (Acts 3:8).

Stood, walked, and *entered* are all past tense. They qualify as parallel construction. But the most lyrically effective example is: *walking, leaping,* and *praising* (all using the "ing" form of the verb). It is a pleasingly balanced sequence. Think how rough the sentence would sound if it ended with, "he was walking, he leapt and praised."

4. "Things worth remembering: the love of God, the power of God, and the plan of God." "The _____ of God" is repeated, and a noun fills in the blank space each time.

5. *"The law of the LORD is perfect, converting the soul: the testimony of the LORD is sure, making wise the simple. The statutes of the LORD are right, rejoicing the heart: the commandment of the LORD is pure, enlightening the eyes"* (Psalm 19:7–8). In these verses, we see this pattern: "The __(noun)__ of the LORD is/are __(adjective)__, 'ing' verb form, the __(noun)__."

6. These chapter titles start with a verb in the same tense: <u>Choose</u> the Message, <u>Organize</u> the Message, <u>Create</u> Memorable Wording.

Parallel construction creates a smooth flow, a feeling of balance, and lovely language that will increase the inspirational level of your message.

OPPOSITES

#1 Single Opposites (Antonyms)

We often see two words of opposite meaning put in the same sentence to contrast thoughts.

1. *"Depart from <u>evil</u>, and do <u>good</u>"* (Psalm 34:14).

2. *"<u>Hatred</u> stirreth up strifes: but <u>love</u> covereth all sins"* (Proverbs 10:12).

3. Life <u>rises</u> and <u>falls</u> on the decisions we make.

4. *"And whosoever will <u>lose</u> his life for my sake shall <u>find</u> it"* (Matthew 16:25).

5. When <u>fear</u> knocks on your door, let <u>faith</u> answer.

In the book *A Tale of Two Cities*, Charles Dickens' opening paragraph is a memorable series of opposites. "It was the best of times, it was the worst of times, it was the age of wisdom, it was the age of foolishness, it was the epoch of belief, it was the epoch of incredulity, it was the season of Light, it was the season of Darkness, it was the spring of hope, it was the winter of despair, we had everything before us, we had nothing before us…"

#2 Double Opposites (Double Antithesis)

Another way to use opposites is to put two words in the first half of the sentence that each have an opposite in the second half.

1. A little boy, who was sitting in a chair in the corner because he was being disciplined, said, "I may be sitting down on the outside, but I'm standing up on the inside!"

2. Your choices will lead you to life and blessings or death and destruction.

3. If you agree with the thoughts of the enemy, you will become weak; but if you agree with the thoughts of God, you will become strong.

4. "*See, I have set before thee this day life and good, and death and evil*" (Deuteronomy 30:15).

#3 Conceptual Opposites and the Use of Contrast

Sometimes instead of using antonyms, we contrast two ideas. We use opposite concepts.

1. "*We walk by faith, not by sight*" (2 Corinthians 5:7).

2. "Problems are not our problems. It's not what happens to you, but what happens in you that matters."[3]

3. "Your friends will stretch your vision or choke your dream."[4]

4. "You make a living from what you get, but you make a life from what you give."[5]

#4 Reverse-Word-Order Antithesis

In this kind of antithesis, you use some of the same words in the first half of the sentence as you do in the second half, but you *reverse the word order* in the second half. So the order of the words is what is opposite.

1. "Let us never negotiate out of fear, but let us never fear to negotiate." (John F. Kennedy) In the first half of this sentence, *negotiate* precedes *fear*. In the second half, the word order is reversed so that *fear* precedes *negotiate*.

2. *I owed a debt I could not pay; He paid a debt He did not owe.* In the first phrase, *owed* precedes *pay*. In the second phrase, *paid* precedes *owe*.

3. *People don't care how much you know, until they know how much you care.* *Care* and *know* switch positions in the second half of the sentence.

4. *"for everyone that exalteth himself shall be abased* [humbled]; *and he that humbleth himself shall be exalted"* (Luke 18:14). *Exalteth* precedes *abased* (humbled), and then *humbleth* precedes *exalted*.

RHYMES

Rhyming words have the same sounds in at least the last syllable of the word. Therefore, a vowel sound will always be included. The rhyming parts of the words do not have to be spelled identically, but the sounds must be identical. For instance, "care" and "stair" rhyme.

Examples of rhyming: Are you playing the <u>blame</u> <u>game</u>? Tell your <u>story</u>, and give God <u>glory</u>. Go to the <u>throne</u>, not the <u>phone</u>. Where God <u>guides</u>, He <u>provides</u>. Let's develop an <u>attitude</u> of <u>gratitude</u>. Jesus came to <u>reverse</u> the <u>curse</u> and set you free.

Rhyming creates a musicality that helps people remember.

PREPARATORY STATEMENTS

I love preparatory statements. They help people grab onto what is most important. To emphasize certain information, use preparatory wording to make your next statement stand out.

The writer of the book of Hebrews used a preparatory statement in 8:1 when he essentially said, "Now here's the main point." Using a preparatory statement gets people ready to listen.

1. "If you don't get anything else today, get this: _____."
2. "Here's the important thing: _____."
3. "Now listen carefully: _____."
4. "Remember, _____."
5. "My word to you today is: _____."

Complete examples of preparatory statements:

- "Remember this: God loves you!"
- "Grab onto this: Forgiveness is the door to freedom!"

ADAPTATION OF A WELL-KNOWN SAYING

You can also get people's attention and help their memories by taking a well-known saying and changing it to fit your message. One minister said, "We're not getting a face lift. We're getting a faith lift." Another said, "At this time of Thanksgiving, are you thanks living?"

COMBINATIONS OF WORD-CRAFTING TOOLS

Many times, preachers use two or more memorable-wording techniques in the same statement.

- Alliteration and Rule of Three: *We have the precious, powerful, protecting blood of Jesus.*

- Parallel Construction and Opposites: *The devil is the author of fear and death. God is the author of faith and life.*
- Reverse-Word-Order Antithesis and Parallel Construction: *Prayer lets you speak to God; meditation lets God speak to you.*[6] (Rick Warren)

A famous example of multiple word-crafting tools is the prayer attributed to St. Francis of Assisi, the thirteenth-century Franciscan Roman Catholic. Notice his use of opposites, repetition, and parallelism.

> LORD, make me an instrument of your peace.
> Where there is hatred, let me sow love,
> Where there is injury, pardon,
> Where there is discord, harmony,
> Where there is doubt, faith,
> Where there is despair, hope,
> Where there is darkness, light,
> Where there is sadness, joy.
> Oh, Divine Master,
> Grant that I may not so much seek to be consoled, as to console,
> To be understood, as to understand,
> To be loved, as to love.
> For it is in giving that we receive;
> It is in pardoning that we are pardoned,
> And it is in dying that we are born to eternal life.

The Holy Spirit used powerful memorable-wording tools in the Bible. Effective communication is the same, no matter what language you speak or in what time of history you live.

Most effective preachers use word-crafting techniques, but we should note that ineffective preachers use them also. I have heard messages using memorable wording that were uninspired, unanointed, and unscriptural. Word-crafting tools are not a substitute for a Scriptural message made alive by the Holy Spirit. But when used correctly, they are part of the art form of preaching.

SECTION V

SHORT-TERM PREPARATION

CHAPTER 24

THE WEEK BEFORE THE MESSAGE

Many seasoned speakers could entertain you for hours with stories that fit the category of, "You won't believe what went wrong! If I had only…"

You might hear comments like these:

- "When I put on my suit, I discovered the cleaners had shrunk it."
- "I forgot the adaptor for a two-prong electrical outlet…"
- "Right before the audience arrived, I plugged in the computer, but…"
- "As I stepped onto the platform, I found I had the wrong message in my hand."

You can prevent many difficulties if you use the week before the message to organize and attend to details.

FOLLOW CLOTHING AND APPEARANCE GUIDELINES

People will judge you first by what you look like. Your appearance will engender trust and respect or the opposite. Be conservative in style and color of clothing. As a general rule, dress a bit more formally than the audience members (unless you are a youth pastor and you dress casually for the sake of connection).

Wear clothing that fits properly. If it is too tight, don't wear it. Your clothing should be loose enough to allow you to gesture without restriction and breathe deeply with ease. Women: Make sure your neckline is high enough and your skirt length long enough. Men: Your tie and collar need to be a little loose for throat expansion as you preach.

If you use a lavalier microphone, your outfit needs to have a lapel, suit jacket, tie, necklace, scarf, or other object onto which you can clip the microphone. If it is a cordless lavalier mic, you need a stiff waistband or belt onto which you can clip the transmitter box.

You can reduce your stress by choosing your clothing in advance.

Hair

Keep your hair off your face and out of your eyes. People want to see your face. If you have a mustache, keep it trimmed so your lips are visible.

Jewelry

Be conservative. Flashy or noisy jewelry or swinging earrings can distract.

Speaking in Other Countries

Research what clothing is appropriate and dress accordingly. I saw a video of Marilyn Hickey preaching in Pakistan to thousands of people. She wore traditional Pakistani clothing, including having her head covered.

ORGANIZE SUPPLIES

Make a checklist of all supplies you will need in the meeting room.

Machinery and Visual Aids

If you are speaking at your own meeting and you are in charge, check the working order of all machinery: computer, overhead projector, microphones, etc. Bring extension cords and adaptors. Check your visual aids: flip chart, videos, props, and PowerPoint. Bring extra bulbs, batteries, markers, etc. Check the lights and temperature settings.

If you are a guest speaker, ask what kind of microphone you will be using. Ask if they have a back-up mic if the first one malfunctions.

Message

Bring your note cards, outline, or manuscript. Bring an extra copy. Bring your Bible.

Introduction

If you write an introduction for your introducer to read, start each new sentence at the left side of the page. Bring two copies in large print.

Personal Items, Giveaway Items, and Product Items

Gather the personal items you will need (cough drops, water bottle, tissue for nose blowing, handkerchief for perspiration, etc.) Gather items to give away and products to sell.

BECOME FAMILIAR WITH THE LOCATION

If possible, go see the room where you will be preaching. If you become familiar with the surroundings, your stress will decrease. Stand in the spot from which you will be speaking. Look out over the seating area. Picture yourself going through the entire speaking process: introduction, standing, behavior before speaking, speaking, leaving the pulpit, sitting, and behavior after being seated. See yourself being confident and focused. You are less likely to feel awkward if you have thought things out ahead of time.

Picture yourself comfortably and joyfully speaking to the group of people. Say, "I belong here. Lord, you have work for me to do, and I'm here to do it. Thank you for this opportunity to serve."

Do a Safety Check

Notice the layout of the room. Look for safety hazards. Are there cords across the floor or throw rugs you could trip over? Does the stage have a sharp drop into the audience? Notice how close the edge of the stage is to where you will stand. Decide ahead of time how much distance you will keep between your feet and the edge. (Yes, it is true. Speakers have fallen off the stage.)

Notice the exits. While you are speaking, you are the leader. In case of a fire or other emergency, you must deal with it or hand the microphone to the appropriate leader. Be ready to respond to surprise events.

Reduce Visual Distractions

If you will be speaking in a classroom, look at the chalkboards. Are they covered with writing? Ask if you can erase them, especially if they are behind you. Are there windows? Pull the drapes shut. Is there an animal in a cage your audience will see when they look at you? Ask if it can be moved. There is nothing like being upstaged by a hamster running on a wheel or a snake slithering along its glass enclosure. Seek to eliminate possible distractions.

ARRANGE THE SEATING

The seating arrangement can help create intimacy, group connection, and warmth, or it can promote isolation and disconnection.

The Psychology of Seating

If you have a large room and only a few people show up, they may think they are in the wrong place and that nothing important will happen. They may feel lonely or isolated and decide they made a mistake in coming. The energy in the audience will be low.

The wrong seating or size of the room can make preaching hard work. It is difficult to maintain eye contact and connect when there are only a few people scattered around a large room. Most experienced speakers would choose a small room filled to overflowing, rather than a large room that is half-full. A shoulder-to-shoulder crowd creates energy and positive expectation.

What Can You Do?

Ask ahead of time: How many people are expected? How big is the room? How many chairs are there? If you are able to influence the seating arrangements, consider these suggestions:

1. If the audience will be small, try to change to a small room.

2. Arrange the seating in advance. After people are seated, they don't like to move.

3. If you are presenting in a large room or auditorium and it is not expected to fill up, you can use masking tape to block entrance into the back seats. Your goal is to make the listeners sit close to you and close to each other.

4. In a room with movable chairs, remove some if a small group is expected. Be ready to add the chairs back if necessary.

5. At a lunch meeting, some people may be seated at tables with their backs to you. After eating, suggest to them they may want to turn their seats to see you. Give them time to do it.

6. Look at the chair arrangement. Think of what is comfortable for the audience. Do the outside chairs need to be slanted toward the speaker so the people on the outside don't get stiff necks?

FINISH YOUR PREPARATION ON THE DAY OF THE MESSAGE

Early Morning Exercise

If you have a lot of energy, exercise can calm you and reduce nervousness, but be careful not to hurt yourself. Caution: If exercise exhausts you, save it for another day.

Put Supplies in Place

Put these at the lectern ahead of time: a glass or bottle of water, cough drop, tissue for nose blowing, handkerchief (for perspiration), props, visual aids, and giveaway items. Don't put your things at the lectern the day before; someone may clean the room. Don't leave your Bible or your message there. Keep them with you.

The Before-Speaking Routine

If possible, do the Before-Speaking Routine less than one hour before you speak.

Test the Microphone

If this is your meeting, test the microphone by speaking into it before the audience arrives. Right before you begin your message, *gently* touch the top of it with your finger to make sure it is on.

CHAPTER 25

FIVE WAYS TO DELIVER A MESSAGE

I know you have seen him—a preacher who walks comfortably around the stage, talking with ease and enthusiasm. His message tumbles out of him with passion. Not only does the message matter to him, but it appears to be part of his very being as if he lives and breathes it.

Should you strive for this kind of presentation? Your abilities are unique to you. You may or may not be able to learn to present like the above preacher. Here's the important thing: there are no rigid rules as to how you must present a message. As you preach, you will develop your own style. And hopefully, you will work with yourself to become the best preacher you can be.

SPEAK FROM NOTE CARDS OR AN OUTLINE

The large majority of speakers will be most effective if they preach from note cards or an outline that contains main-idea words or phrases—not sentences. (If you write sentences, you will be tempted to read them.) The beauty of this presentation method is you have notes to help your memory, but you speak extemporaneously. You have prepared (and hopefully practiced aloud), but you choose the sentence structure as you speak. This creates freshness and vitality.

It helps to highlight key words in yellow or circle them. Keep a lot of white space and use large print. Start each new concept or phrase at the left hand margin, and don't use all capital letters.

When you need to glance at your outline or notes, look down, grab the words with your brain, look up, pause, make eye contact, and then speak. Don't start talking while you are still looking down. Carry a duplicate of your outline in case the first one gets damaged.

Memorize the opening, transitions, closing, and any stories. As you become proficient in using this method, you might naturally transition into the next one.

MEMORIZE MAIN IDEAS AND SPEAK EXTEMPORANEOUSLY

You may be able to memorize the main points and speak extemporaneously. In this method, you have not memorized a word-for-word message, but you may have written one. Or you may have written an outline with the opening, closing, body and supporting information. The point is, this is not impromptu preaching. You will have prepared (and probably practiced aloud).

SPEAK IMPROMPTU

Impromptu speaking means speaking without preparation. I don't recommend this as a regular practice. But you may be at a meeting when the preacher says to you, "Would you come up and say a few words?"

When you speak impromptu, you can still have an opening, body, and closing. But don't put your focus there. Just say what you think you should say.

MEMORIZE A WORD-FOR-WORD MANUSCRIPT

Professional speakers often memorize a word-for-word manuscript. They are experts at sounding spontaneous. It is *not* a good idea for most preachers to memorize their messages word for word.

Drawbacks to memorizing the message word for word:

- Many preachers don't have the discipline to write a word-for-word message.

- Many preachers don't have time (or the ability) to memorize a message.

- Memorized messages tend to look stilted and unnatural, and they may hinder relationship with the listeners.
- It is easy to forget an important part.
- This method does not allow you to yield to Holy Spirit inspiration.

READ A WORD-FOR-WORD MANUSCRIPT

This is the least desirable delivery method. The speaker's eyes tend to stay focused on the page. Reading blocks relationship. It also bores people.

I do *not* recommend it, but if you are determined to read from a manuscript, here are presentation tips to help you:

1. Print out the message in large print.
2. Start every new sentence at the left margin.
3. Memorize the opening and closing sentences so you can speak them directly to the audience.
4. Look at the audience while you say the last three or four words in a sentence.
5. Maintain eye contact at the end of the sentence for a moment. Pause. Don't look down to your script too soon, or it can trivialize the words you just spoke.
6. Make an effort to be animated and enthusiastic.
7. Look at the listeners whenever possible.

The only time I recommend reading a word-for-word manuscript is if your words may have legal consequences.

As you gain experience in public speaking, you will learn what works best for you. If your delivery method blocks connection, try something different until you develop your own effective style.

CHAPTER 26

HOW TO PRACTICE DELIVERY OF THE MESSAGE

The student preacher walked confidently to the lectern and began preaching with passion. He spoke clearly and intensely. The subject obviously mattered to him. He looked like he loved being up there. But in the middle of one of his sentences, the preaching instructor held up his hand and said, "Time's up."

The preacher replied, "But wait! I haven't preached the message yet. I'm not even finished with my opening!"

What could have helped this beginning preacher discover ahead of time that his message was too long? He needed to practice the delivery out loud and time it.

Practice the Before-Speaking Routine

Learn the warm-up routine and use it. It will eliminate many presentation problems and free you up to concentrate on God, the people, and the message you have for them.

HOW TO PRACTICE THE MESSAGE

Speakers' Mistakes

Some speakers don't practice at all, or they make the mistake of rehearsing in their heads and not out loud. When Billy Graham was a student preacher, he practiced his messages in an empty church building. Sometimes he would paddle a canoe out to an island where he walked around preaching boldly.[1] Speak your message aloud. There is no substitute for a verbal practice time.

Questions to Ask Yourself

When you practice, analyze your delivery. Ask yourself: Is my voice too loud or too soft? Am I speaking too fast or too slowly? Am I pronouncing the words clearly? Am I pausing at the right places? Are my gestures natural? Do I have any distracting vocal or physical habits? Does my posture give the message that I am confident? Am I using eye contact? Do the ideas flow and make sense? Does this message matter to me? Does it *sound* like this message matters to me?

Practice Holding a Microphone

Hold an object, like a hairbrush, in microphone position as you rehearse. Watch in the mirror. Keep the "microphone" in front of your chin.

Time the Delivery

If you have tight time parameters, add or delete material during practice until the timing is correct.

Get Feedback on Your Delivery

- Audio record your message. Listen to it and evaluate.
- Videotape yourself. You can increase your skill levels rapidly if you see yourself speaking. A friend of mine had a videotaped class assignment in college. She was shocked to see how stern she looked as she scowled at the camera. Whenever she made a point, she tapped her knuckle on the table. She had no idea how she came across until she saw herself on video.
- Practice in front of a mirror.
- Practice in front of people. Ask friends or family to listen. Ask for positive suggestions. You can also go to a public-speaking coach.

Your Last Practice

For the final practice, use the exact notes, outline, or manuscript you will use when you present. If you will be preaching in a new outfit, practice in it, including the shoes you plan to wear.

PRACTICE YIELDING TO THE INSPIRATIONAL HOLY SPIRIT FLOW

You have probably seen preachers who take a Scripture and "run with it." They do a free-form kind of Holy Spirit-inspired delivery. It is as if they have grabbed a football and are running for a touchdown. There is excitement and Holy Spirit power in it. They have learned to step into the inspirational flow of the Holy Spirit.

How Can You Practice Getting Into This Inspirational Flow?

Take a Scripture and meditate on it. Read it and speak it. Let it sink into your spirit. Declare that it is true. Explain the rightness of the Scripture to yourself out loud. Let the support Scriptures and your life experiences that demonstrate the truth of the Scripture tumble out of you. Be bold in proclaiming its truth.

Preach to the furniture. Preach to the walls. Preach to your tool bench. If God's Word is alive on the inside of you and you have a speaking-for-God call upon your life, you will have a desire to tell about God's goodness. Just start talking. Talk to the LORD and explain to Him why you believe the Scripture. Go into great detail. Become fervent.

If your anointing is that of a teacher, I am not suggesting you need to preach like this. I am only saying that this practice can help prime the pump and develop your preaching ability.

SECTION VI

DELIVERING THE MESSAGE

INTRODUCTION

One Sunday morning, I visited a church where the pastor's wife opened the service with announcements. Then she transitioned into Scriptural encouragements. When she left the lectern, I said to the person next to me, "She's a good speaker."

The person replied, "Now she is, but you should have seen her three years ago. She was so terrified that she would tremble and cry as she spoke. She's come a long way."

Even if public speaking and preaching do not come easily to you, you too can become an effective speaker. Before we take a look at delivery techniques, let us consider our delivery goals.

Delivery Goals

When we think about delivering a message, certain goals remain constant. We want to be natural (not stilted) and confident (not insecure). We want to pronounce words clearly so people hear our words accurately. We want to be authentic and conversational. We want to use simple language and a logical progression of ideas. We want to connect with our listeners in a way that shows we care about them. We want to persuade our listeners to apply the message to their lives and deepen their relationship with God.

In their book *The Elements of Preaching*, Warren and David Wiersbe said: "Good delivery does not attract attention to itself. It is simply a tool, wisely used, to get the truth of the Word into the hearts of people."[1]

In his book *Expository Preaching with Word Pictures*, Jack Hughes comments about the importance of delivery:

> As I preached and taught the Word, I soon realized that the method of delivery was also very important. I needed to learn how to deliver the Word in such a way that it held people's attention, gave them understanding, and helped them remember. I needed to preach to the heart. It was then that I began my quest for insight. I began to look at well-known expositors and asked myself, "What is it about their preaching that makes them so effective?"[2]

CHAPTER 27

EVALUATE YOUR READINESS TO PREACH

When you think you are ready to preach, use the Basic Preaching Statement to evaluate your preparedness.

> **Basic Preaching Statement**
>
> When you preach, it is important that you care about the people and meet their needs by delivering a Scriptural message, with sincerity, in your own unique way, as you follow the lead of the Holy Spirit.

Care about the people.

Do you respect the listeners and care about their well-being? Do God's concerns for them beat in your heart? Have you prayed for the compassion of Jesus to flow through you? Do you know how to communicate that you care about them?

Meet their needs.

Do you know their needs and challenges? Does your message address a need?

Make the message Scriptural.

Have you researched your main Scriptures? Have you followed the principles of Bible interpretation? Do your beliefs and opinions agree with Scripture?

Be sincere.

Do you believe what you are going to preach? Is it alive in you? Do you believe it will help people?

Use your own unique speaking style.

Speak in a way that is natural to you. Don't try to perform or use a "preaching voice." Don't copy someone else's preaching style. Let the best part of you be visible as you preach.

Follow the lead of the Holy Spirit.

Are you spiritually ready? Is there anything you need to repent for? Have you put aside all distractions? Have you prayed? Do you have any personal agenda you need to let go of? Have you laid aside all worry? To the best of your knowledge, have you been obedient? Are you focused on God's message and the answer He has for the listeners' needs? Are you trusting and expecting God to lead you, strengthen you, and work through you as you preach?

After doing the preaching statement evaluation, also check the preparation areas already mentioned. Is your message organized? Do you know your bottom-line statement? Do you know what you want the listeners to *know* and *do*? Have you practiced out loud?

If you learn the public speaking skills on the following pages, they will help you deliver your message with sincerity in your own unique way. And they will help give you freedom to follow the lead of the Holy Spirit.

CHAPTER 28

GRAMMAR AND PRONUNCIATION GUIDELINES

Many years ago, public-speaking teachers emphasized perfect enunciation, lovely vocal tone, and excellent grammar. They taught a formal delivery based on details of vocal production, rather than emphasizing content, influence, rapport with the audience, integrity, and a natural delivery which we favor today. Because of that old-fashioned teaching, some people think public-speaking training will create a phony and pretentious preacher. Nothing could be further from the truth. The following grammar and pronunciation guidelines can help you connect with your listeners and accomplish God's purpose for your message.

GRAMMAR GUIDELINES

#1 Use Simple, Conversational Language

Toss formal grammar out if it prevents you from being natural. For example, you don't need to say, "From whom did you get the book?" Just say, "Who did you get the book from?" Be natural—not stiff or formal.

#2 Use Phrases Occasionally

You don't need to speak in complete sentences all the time. Sometimes the simplicity of a phrase or one-word exclamation has more impact. Examples: "Absolutely." "No doubt about it."

#3 Speak in Complete Thoughts

Complete sentences are not always necessary, but it is important to speak in complete thoughts. Some speakers are hard to follow because they start a sentence, then stop in the middle and switch to talking about something else.

If you organize and practice your message out loud ahead of time, you can avoid the scattered thinking that starts a sentence and then changes mid-stream to a different one.

#4 Avoid Awkward Language

Don't use "yourself" instead of "you" or "ourselves" instead of "us." Examples: Don't say, "Just like yourself" or "Just like ourselves." Instead, say, "Just like you" or "Just like us."

#5 Secular Speaking Versus Preaching

In many secular, professional-speaking situations, the speaker who makes grammatical errors will be discredited in the eyes of the audience. But in preaching, correct grammar is not a requirement. Some very effective preachers don't use correct grammar. It has not held them back. If you do not use perfect grammar, don't be intimidated. God called you because He wants *you* up there speaking. God needs all kinds of preachers because He has all kinds of people. There is a place for everyone in God's workforce.

PRONUNCIATION GUIDELINES

One of my friend's pastors preached about Jesus washing the disciples' feet. The preacher said Jesus used "that damp cloth." But he did not pronounce the "p" clearly. Several people in the congregation thought he had said "damn." Our goal regarding pronunciation is to be understood. We want to speak clearly in a natural way.

#1 Don't Drop the Last Syllable or Word

Some speakers reduce their volume and lower their pitch on the last syllable, word, or last couple of words in their sentences. This is called "dropping" or "swallowing" words.

Record yourself talking. Are the ending syllables spoken too softly or not at all? Your listeners want to hear your words.

In some dialects, the speaker routinely omits the last syllable of multi-syllabic words or even the last word. If the listeners and speaker use the same dialect, it is fine because the dialect then does not block comprehension.

Inadequate breath support can also cause you to drop ending syllables or words. You can correct this by doing the following:

- Learn abdominal breathing. Practice breathing deeply with your stomach expanding like a balloon.
- Learn to pause and breathe so you don't run out of air at the end of your sentences.

If you have a habit of dropping ending syllables, you can retrain yourself. Read aloud and exaggerate your pronunciation. Keep your volume up at the end of sentences.

#2 Help People Understand Your Dialect

If you speak in a different dialect than your audience, slow down and speak distinctly. Ask God to help your listeners understand your words.

#3 Identify and Change Your Habitual Mispronunciations

Ask your friends if there are words you regularly mispronounce. If there are, learn to say them correctly.

- Sometimes people combine words to create new, incorrect ones. I have heard people combine the words "fluster" and "frustrate" to create "flustrated" or "flustration."
- Sometimes people change the order of one sound within a word as in "preception" for "perception" or "revelant" for "relevant."
- Sometimes people add sounds to words as in "forestration" for "forestation."

Mispronouncing words will distract some of your audience and will not help your credibility. Get feedback. Give someone the right to correct you.

#4 Handling Occasional Mispronunciations While You Preach

If you mispronounce words that you know how to say:

1. Slow down.
2. If it was minor, continue speaking.
3. If it was major, correct it.
4. Pause to collect yourself and then continue.

#5 Prevent Mispronunciations

You cannot prevent all mispronunciations, but you can eliminate a good number of them if you follow these suggestions:

1. Rehearse your message out loud.
2. Warm up your voice and articulators before you preach.
3. If you are speaking fast, slow down.

If your pronunciation is not easily understandable, work to correct it.

CHAPTER 29

VOCAL PATTERNS WHILE PREACHING

One Christmas Eve, I visited a church where the minister spoke normally for the announcements. But when he began his message, he adopted a strange, singsong voice. His volume and pitch went up and down in a monotonous, predictable pattern that didn't have anything to do with the meaning of his message. It was a mindless, memorized pattern of religious speaking. As I watched him, I realized there must be a lot of preachers like him because he sounded like a parody of a preacher found in the routines of some comedians.

BASIC SPEAKING INSTRUCTION REGARDING VOCAL PATTERNS

#1 Mention the Obvious

If there is something unusual about you that the audience will wonder about, explain it to them. I heard a professional speaker whose face was badly scarred tell his audience, "I was in a fire." A minister who had a face lift said to her audience, "Some of you may be wondering: *Did she?* Yes. I did have work done on my face." The goal here is to help the audience pay attention to the message and not be distracted by extraneous details.

#2 Speak Conversationally

Don't put phony drama into your voice. Don't try to speak in a "preacher's voice." Talk normally.

#3 Speak Clearly and Distinctly

Don't slur your words.

#4 Be Yourself

Effective speakers develop their own styles. They don't copy anyone. Be your best self, and your own style will develop.

#5 Avoid Filler Sounds and Words

Don't fill the air space with sounds or words that don't move the message forward. Avoid saying: *uh, well, um, and, you know, see, you see, okay,* or *know what I mean?*

Some speakers are not aware of their habit of using filler words or sounds. They may even use *praise God, hallelujah,* or *amen* as filler words. I heard a missionary whose message was excellent, but it was marred by her repetitive use of "Amen?" She said, "Amen?" after every other sentence. It was disruptive. Learn the difference between nervously filling the air with these words versus Holy Spirit-led use of them. Filler words are time wasters. Let the silence be silence.

HOW YOUR ANOINTING MAY AFFECT YOUR VOCAL PATTERN

Your anointing will affect your delivery style. As a general statement, the people anointed as teachers explain the Word. They may speak with a calm, quiet, and steady style. The people with a preaching anointing announce the Word. They tend to be louder and more dramatic. The people with the anointing of an evangelist are often intense, dramatic, and bold. Many preachers have a combination of these styles with a tendency toward one or the other.

Some preachers shout, thinking that loudness demonstrates the anointing. Yelling is not a sign of the anointing or a substitute for it. A God-inspired message can be soft, medium, or loud. It may be all three.

HOW TO USE VOCAL VARIETY

Do you remember the saying "Variety is the spice of life?" Vocal variety is important. Vary your rate, pitch, volume, tone, and intensity. Learn to pause effectively. Vocal variety will help keep your listeners interested.

#1 Rate of Speech

People speak at different rates of speed. Find out if your normal speech is fast, medium, or slow. To identify your rate, speak normally into a recorder for one minute. Then listen to it and count the number of words. A medium rate is about 150 words per minute.

Rate of speech is important because:

- People usually feel most comfortable with others who speak at their own rate.
- People think at different speeds. Some people think slower, some faster. I am not talking about intelligence. I am referring to the brain's processing speed.

Problems with speaking too fast: Some listeners will not have time to process and react. Speaking fast may decrease the clarity of your pronunciation.

If you speak to a large group, you may need to speak slower to avoid an echo effect caused by poor acoustics. Also, slowing down will help your listeners hear your words when there is a noise.

If you speak too fast, how can you slow down?

- Breathe deeply.
- Pause after phrases and at the end of sentences.

Key Recommendation: Vary the speed of your delivery. Most of the time, use a medium rate. Every now and then, speed up or slow down.

#2 Pitch

Pitch has to do with how high or low a sound is. If you don't vary your pitch, you will speak in a monotone. Listen to variations in pitch as people talk. Our voices go up in pitch at the end of a question and down at the end of a sentence.

Notice your normal pitch level. Our voices often rise in pitch when we are angry, when we are nervous, or when we yell. High voices can be uncomfortable to listen to. When the anointing is strong, some preachers shout—which raises their pitch. Keep your pitch from rising too high when you preach.

Tips on how to lower your pitch:

- Breathe deeply (inconspicuously).
- Slow down.
- Reduce your volume (speak quieter).

The goal is to speak at your natural pitch level with variation and in a way that is comfortable for the audience to hear. Speakers can develop voice problems if they habitually speak at a pitch that is too low or too high.

#3 Volume

Some preachers shout in their attempt to hold people's attention or in an effort to drive home a point. Some shout because they think it proves they are passionate about their message. Shouting can backfire; you can wear people out. I bought a recording of a meeting, but after listening to fifteen minutes of it, I threw it out. I don't like being shouted at nonstop.

Other preachers speak too softly, almost at a whisper. Some of their listeners cannot hear the words.

If you speak without a microphone, or if the group is large, speak slower. Enunciate clearly. Sometimes slow, clear speech can make up for a lack of volume.

How to make your voice louder:

1. Do vocal warm-ups ahead of time so the full power of your voice is available to you.

2. Open your mouth wider.
3. Breathe deeply.
4. Stand up straight with your chest lifted. Don't sit.
5. Keep your head up.
6. Speak at a moderate speed, with some slowing down. Don't speak fast.
7. Aim your voice at a person in the back row.

Key Recommendation: Vary your volume. Use a lot of medium volume and then a softer or louder statement.

#4 Whispering

Some speech teachers recommend whispering to get the listeners' attention. It can be effective (especially with children), but there is a problem. When you whisper or speak softly, some listeners will not hear you. Therefore, if you whisper, repeat the statement using your regular voice.

#5 Tone

Tone of voice conveys an emotion. You can say "I like this" with a tone that is critical, sarcastic, warm, or happy. Your tone of voice will tell people about you. Listen to yourself speak. What is your tone conveying?

#6 Intensity

Intensity involves the extremeness of your expression. When you are ardently focused, profoundly serious, or exceptionally emotional, you are demonstrating intensity. A low-key, lackadaisical delivery will bore people. A relentless driving force might exhaust them. In a natural delivery, most preachers will vary their intensity.

#7 Pauses

Pauses are one of your most important tools. They can mean the difference between being effective or not. As you speak, your listeners respond with their thoughts. When you pause, you give them time to think.

When should you pause?

1. Before your opening
2. Before or after a thought unit or phrase
3. Before and after an important point
4. After you ask a question
5. After a preparation statement: "Now here's the main point." (Pause)
6. When shifting from one section of the message to another
7. When you need to breathe
8. When the audience is clapping or laughing
9. When there is an unexpected noise, like an airplane overhead
10. Anytime you want to emphasize something

Begin your message with a pause. Don't start until you have the attention of your audience. Don't let silence scare you.

#8 Interesting Vocalization

Some preachers use singing and/or descriptive sounds to increase the interest level of their messages.

Singing

One morning I listened to a preacher talk about Jesus and Zacchaeus, the tax collector. When the pastor got to Luke 19:3, he sang, "And a wee, little man was he." I thought I had been paying attention. But when he sang, my brain zoomed back from wherever it had been.

Singing a phrase grabs people's attention and adds fun. If you can sing mostly on key, sing a phrase of a song now and then.

Sound Effects

Another way to add interest and fun is to add sound effects while you tell a story. I saw a minister illustrate his point with an anecdote about riding his motorcycle. He walked slowly across the stage, his hands in position as if holding the handlebars. He interspersed guttural motorcycle sounds with his dialogue. The audience loved it. It provided a welcome relief from the seriousness of the message. But it did not diminish the bottom-line of his teaching.

Adding sound effects occasionally can enrich your listeners' overall experience.

HOW TO AVOID VOICE MISUSE AND VOICE ABUSE

Have you ever gone to a sports event, yelled for your team, and ended up with a sore throat or hoarse voice? Or have you become hoarse or even lost your voice from preaching or singing? If you answered yes, then you have experienced voice misuse or abuse. Voice abuse refers to mistreating the voice or using it in a wrong way.

Professional singers train to develop and protect their voices. Preachers also use their voices professionally, but often they don't have any vocal training. Each of us has different vocal qualities and abilities. What I need to do to protect my voice may be different than what you need to do.

Voice Problems

Think of the unusual voices you have heard. Some are unique and interesting, but others are the result of a voice problem. Some have a strained quality that denotes high stress and tension. Chronic hoarseness, sore throats after singing or preaching, frequent throat clearing, and whispery or gravelly voices can lead to or indicate a medical problem. Vocal nodules, vocal polyps, and paralyzed vocal cords are some of the problems people can develop. It is far preferable to prevent these situations rather than to undergo surgery or be told there is no treatment available.

Typical Causes of Voice Problems

1. Habitually speaking at the wrong pitch
2. Using too much volume (yelling)
3. Placing the sound in the wrong area (i.e., placing the sound in the back of the throat instead of in the nose and mouth area)
4. Neglecting to use abdominal breath support

How to Protect Your Voice

1. Always do vocal warm-ups before you speak in public.
2. Use a microphone.
3. Learn the limits of your voice and abide by them. Don't do anything that results in hoarseness.
4. Use abdominal breathing. It will take pressure off your throat.
5. Stay mostly in your natural pitch range.
6. Don't shout for long periods of time.
7. Place your vocal sound in the mask area of the face (nose and mouth area).
8. Do regular vocal exercises to extend your vocal range.
9. Have room-temperature or warm water available when you preach.
10. Stand up straight.
11. While singing with the congregation, don't sing at maximum volume. Worship with your heart more than your voice. Save your voice for preaching.
12. Make vocal rest a part of your lifestyle. Don't talk, sing, or whisper for periods of time.
13. Don't converse in noisy environments where you have to shout to be heard (i.e., noisy restaurants, sports events, or loud musical performances).
14. Stay hydrated. Drink plenty of water the two days before you preach.

If you have a problem with voice abuse, get professional help. Some singing teachers and speech pathologists do voice therapy. Also, go to a doctor who is a throat specialist.

You may want to read books on the care of your voice.

- *Winning With Your Voice* by Morton Cooper. Cooper is a speech pathologist with a strong background in voice therapy.
- *Vocal Workout* and *Maximum Vocal Performance* by Christopher Beatty. Beatty is a vocal coach.
- *Power in the Pulpit: How to Prepare and Deliver Expository Sermons* by Jerry Vines and Jim Shaddix. This book has a section on voice use and abuse.

Educate yourself and work to maintain a healthy voice. It is not a blessing to be a preacher who cannot speak. You are the temple of the Holy Spirit. Taking care of your body includes taking care of your vocal cords.

HOW TO READ SCRIPTURE ALOUD

The most common mistake is reading too fast. I have heard preachers race through their reading of Scripture. Even though I was familiar with the verses, I could not distinguish the words. If you are going to read Scripture aloud during your message, practice. Read slowly and clearly. Use pauses and vocal variety. Emphasize important words.

Key Recommendation: If you pretend the listeners have never heard the verse before and never will again, you will be more likely to give it the careful reading it deserves.

The suggestions in this chapter are not new or revolutionary. They are basic. You may already use these vocal techniques. But if you don't, there is nothing more fundamental than mastering your speaking patterns and the way you use your voice.

CHAPTER 30

HOW TO USE YOUR BODY DURING THE MESSAGE

Your body language, the gestures you make, and the way you move and stand can help convince your listeners that you are a leader and have something important to say.

PHYSICAL SUGGESTIONS

Stand Up Straight

Stand tall. Hold your head up. Keep your weight balanced on both feet. Don't lean on one foot. You are the ambassador of the King of Glory. You are His representative and His spokesperson. Toss out feelings of low self-worth, inadequacy, or inferiority. Rise up to your position—not in arrogance, but in confidence. In Judges 6:12, the angel of the Lord called Gideon a "mighty man of valour." That is you.

Breathe Deeply

Breathe deeply in an inconspicuous way. Don't let your shoulders rise up or your chest puff out. Pull air into your stomach area. Let your stomach expand like a balloon. When you release the air, the stomach goes back in.

Use Eye Contact

Look at individuals in every section of the audience. Speak directly to them. If you want to increase your energy and confidence, find the smiling faces and speak to them.

Use Appropriate Facial Expressions

Don't smile at inappropriate times. I have seen female speakers smile almost nonstop, even when telling a sad story. Other speakers might not smile at all. Facial expressions should be appropriate to what you are saying.

MOVEMENT AND GESTURES

Goals of Physical Movement

1. Hold people's attention
2. Demonstrate the message
3. Increase relationship connection
4. Reduce trembling in your body

Gestures

Use normal gestures. Using no gesture at all is better than a phony, stiff, or unnatural one. If you are telling a story, you can use larger, more dramatic gestures and movement.

Size of Gestures

If you are speaking only for a video or TV program, you can use small gestures. But if you present to a live group and they are not close to you, use large physical movements. Many of them may not be able to see a small gesture.

Nervous Mannerisms

Have you ever seen a speaker shake the coins in his pocket, stroke his beard or tie, or pace back and forth excessively? Nervous mannerisms will undercut your message. While you preach, pay attention to what your body and hands are doing.

Physicalized Talking

Become physically expressive. Learn to use your body when you preach, especially when you tell a story.

In a message on the importance of paying attention to one's own thoughts, you could say: "You know the story of the fish that got away? In the fisherman's mind it was [*stretch your arms out wide*] this big! But in reality, [*bring your hands in to indicate a much smaller fish*] it was this big. Sometimes we think of our problems in the same way. Our mind says they are [*stretch your arms out wide*] this big! But in reality, they are [*bring your hands in to indicate a much smaller size*] this big. It's important that we pay attention to how our minds are analyzing our current situation."

When you use a physical movement in a story, it will usually precede the words that describe it. Notice that I mentioned the preacher's action before the words that describe the action. First do the action, and then say the words that describe it.

Practice using physicalized talking. What hand and arm movements might you use for these sentences? (1) Let the little children come to me. (2) How would I know? (3) You're not going under; you're going over! (4) Leave it behind!

I am not suggesting you memorize movements for certain sentences. Become more physically expressive. Interesting physical movements can increase audience retention. What good is a message if people don't remember it?

Moving Around

Experienced speakers often move around on the platform, speaking to and looking at different audience members. Also, they may walk into the audience area to create intimacy.

Should all speakers move around? No. Some preachers speak more effectively from behind the lectern. And that is the best place for them.

Don't feel that you have to step away from the lectern in your first presentations. But at some point, leave the safety of the lectern and experiment with movement. How? Walk toward the audience while you talk. Stop. Pause. Look at them. Speak to specific people. Pause. Start talking and walking again while you move toward another section. Repeat the sequence.

If you don't walk around to connect, you can turn to each section of the audience as you speak. Look at them and talk directly to them for a moment. Then shift your gaze to another section. Do this throughout the message.

WHAT TO DO WITH YOUR HANDS WHEN YOU PREACH

Some people feel awkward and don't know what to do with their hands. Hands can stay discreetly out of the way, add interest and impact, or undermine the presentation. Sometimes speakers are not aware of what their hands are doing.

Avoid Distracting Hand Mannerisms

1. Don't fiddle with your clothing, button, tie, necklace, watch, etc.
2. Don't twirl or stroke your mustache.
3. Don't scratch your head or any other part of your body.
4. Don't jab your index finger at people while you talk.

Key Recommendation: Pay attention to what your hands are doing.

During the Presentation

1. Unless there is a natural gesture to be made, don't gesture.
2. When telling a story, you can use larger and more dramatic gestures.
3. Allow your hands to hang at your sides, your palms facing the side of your legs. Your middle knuckles will be slightly bent so the hand is curved. It may not feel natural, but it will look natural.
4. If your hands shake, don't hold papers. Use note cards instead.
5. To reduce the shaking of your hands, use a big, expansive arm movement that fits into what you are saying.

If you do physical warm-ups before speaking, your movements will appear more fluid and natural. As you gain experience in preaching, you will develop more confidence and ease of movement.

CHAPTER 31

BEGINNING THE MESSAGE: WHAT TO DO IN THE FIRST MINUTE

One of the tell-tale signs of beginning speakers is how they start. They may scurry across the platform or begin speaking before they even put their papers on the lectern. They feel pressured to "hurry-up" because everyone is watching and waiting. Their eyes may look anywhere except at the audience. Their behavior demonstrates their discomfort. What you do in the beginning of the message is important.

What to Do in the First Minute

1. While waiting to speak, sit up straight.
2. Don't cross your legs. Crossed legs reduce the blood flow (and oxygen) to your brain.
3. Put a pleasant look on your face.
4. Listen to your introducer.
5. Stand up.
6. As you approach the lectern, walk tall.
7. Smile at your introducer, nod your head toward him in acknowledgment, shake his hand, or hug him. Do whatever is appropriate.

8. Place your materials on the lectern.
9. Face the audience.
10. Stand firmly on both feet.
11. Keep your head up.
12. Look at people. Make eye contact.
13. Smile. You are silently greeting people.
14. Look at different sections of the audience.
15. Breathe deeply two times, inconspicuously.
16. Don't start talking until the audience is quiet and attentive.
17. Begin speaking when you are ready. Don't rush it.
18. Begin with your interesting opening.

In contrast to these suggestions, some pastors chat comfortably while approaching the lectern, but for most speakers it is not the best way to start.

If you follow the above suggestions, they will help you start the relationship between your listeners and you in a positive way.

CHAPTER 32

HOW TO HANDLE THE MICROPHONE

Have you seen these microphone scenarios?

- The preacher's message is interrupted by a loud, high-pitched noise from the sound system.
- The microphone stops working. The speaker continues but cannot be heard.
- The speaker begins talking but does not realize his voice is not being amplified.
- The speaker begins with, "Uh, is this mic on? Can you hear me?"

Should You Use a Microphone?

Yes. A mic gives you the ability to use a greater depth of vocal expression with changes in pitch, tone, and volume. You can speak quietly and still be heard. Using a microphone reduces stress on your throat and vocal cords. Listeners who have a hearing loss can hear you better if you use a mic.

TYPES OF MICROPHONES

#1 Stationary Microphone

Some lecterns have a built-in microphone. Or sometimes the mic is on a metal stand and cannot be detached. Stationary mics can be uncomfortable to use. They require your body to be in a rigid, fixed position. They restrict your physical movement which creates a visually boring presentation. The stationary mic should be pointed at your mouth. It may be up to eight inches away.

Ask about the type of microphone ahead of time.

Adjusting the Stationary Pole Microphone

If the mic is not adjusted to your height, fix it immediately. Unscrew the ring on the pole and raise or lower it. Pause before you begin speaking.

#2 Hand-Held Microphone (Cordless or With Cord)

A hand-held mic lets you move around, but it limits you to one hand and arm for gestures. Hold the mic in front of your chin (or below your chin if you have a big voice). The bottom of the mic should point to the ground. Keep your mic-holding hand in front of the center of your body. Keep your elbow in close to your side. Hold the mic steady in position. Your voice may fade out if you lower the mic.

Don't cover your mouth with the mic. The audience wants to see your mouth. If you laugh, keep the mic down a bit, not up in speaking position. The battery in the cordless mic may go dead while you speak. Have extra batteries available.

#3 Lavalier/Lapel Microphone (Cordless or With Cord)

The lavalier mic clips onto your jacket lapel, tie, scarf, or necklace. If you need to, you can put a string around your neck and hang the mic from it. With lapel mics, if you turn your head to one side and talk, your voice may fade out.

The advantages of a lapel microphone are that you have both hands free, and you can walk around. The cordless lapel mic has a thin wire going from the mic to a transmitter box that clips onto your belt or waistband in back. A belt is preferable. Some waistbands are not stiff enough; the box may fall off.

#4 Headset Microphone

Headset mics wrap around the head or around the ear. A major advantage is that the speaker's voice does not fade in or out as he turns his head. Some people love using headsets. Others don't like the feel of something gripping their head.

TIPS FOR USING A MICROPHONE

If you are providing the microphone, check it the week before and again the day of the presentation.

Test the Microphone Before the Audience Arrives

1. Speak into the mic. Find out how far from your mouth you can hold it and still be heard.

2. Practice turning the mic on and off.

3. With the mic turned on, walk close to the speakers to determine the distance that you need to keep between you and the speakers to avoid feedback noise.

Test the Microphone Again Before You Begin the Message

Right before you begin, gently touch the top of the mic with your finger or fingernail to make sure it is on. (You will hear a slight sound.) The key word is *gently*. Microphones are made to receive sound. They are not made to be hit, thumped, or tapped.

If the Microphone Goes Dead

If the mic goes dead and you are speaking without a mic, look at someone in the back row and speak directly to them. Use deep breathing so your abdominal muscles can project your voice. If the group is large, speak slowly and distinctly. Some speakers can project without a mic and others cannot. Learn your vocal limitations.

Coughing Into a Microphone

If you are using a handheld mic, move the mic away from your mouth when you cough. If you are using a lavalier mic, turn your head away from it, or cover the mic with your hand. If you are wearing a headset mic and you have a repetitive cough, ask the sound person to turn off the mic when you cough.

Avoid the Screech of Feedback Noise

1. When your microphone is on, don't stand in front of a loud speaker that is part of the mic's amplifying system.//
2. Don't point the microphone at the amplifying speaker. You don't want the sound from the speaker going into the mic.
3. If there is a stationary mic at the lectern but you are using a lavalier or hand-held mic, turn off the stationary mic.
4. If you start with one kind of mic and switch to another, turn off the first one.

Safety

Microphones are powered by electricity. They can be dangerous, especially if you are wet or around water. Ask a professional electrical person what you need to do to stay safe.

Be Careful What You Say Around a Microphone

Even if you think the mic is off, monitor your mouth. Some preachers have assumed the mic was off and made negative comments that were broadcast through the speaker system. Avoid embarrassment. Only speak good words. Or don't speak any words at all.

Once your mic is turned on, don't forget it is on. I had a situation where I was sitting silently, waiting to be introduced. The meeting had not started, but I had already turned on my lapel mic because the on/off switch was difficult to access. I did not want to fumble around up at the lectern, trying to turn it on. To be friendly, the lady next to me asked me a question. As I answered, I heard my voice bounce around the room.

In the best-case scenario, you know how to use the mic, and it functions perfectly—giving you the freedom to concentrate on the listeners, the message, and the Holy Spirit.

CHAPTER 33

PRESENTATION MODIFICATIONS FOR SPECIFIC GROUPS

It is important to adapt your message and delivery to fit your listeners. If you preach at a retirement home, you will do a different delivery than if you preach to high school students. If you preach to seven-year-olds, you will need to speak at their level. I have seen speakers preach what would have been good messages if they had known how to adapt their delivery and word choices to the group they were speaking to.

PREACHING WITH AN INTERPRETER

Speak in short sentences or phrases. Pause after each phrase for the interpretation. A phrase-by-phrase rhythm will develop between you and the interpreter. Adjust the length of the message to allow for interpretation time. Show the interpreter your notes ahead of time and pray with him. If he knows where you are headed with the message, he may know how to interpret more effectively. Some languages cannot be translated word for word from our language. Also, it helps if the interpreter is a Christian and knows Scripture.

Use illustrations that apply to all humans or that are specific to the listeners' culture. Avoid using jokes, Greek or Hebrew words, or slang.

Don't look at the interpreter while he interprets. Keep your gaze on the listeners. Just listen for when he stops speaking and then continue. Don't jump in too quickly, or you will both be talking at the same time.

HELP PEOPLE UNDERSTAND YOUR DIALECT

In his book *Just As I Am,* Billy Graham talks about his accent and how difficult it was for some listeners to understand his words. He said, "When I talked at my customary rapid clip, people looked at me curiously, as if my heavily accented drawl were a foreign language."[1] In reference to his preaching in India he said:

> At one point in my address, I knew that I had said something awry. Talking about Jesus, I had said, "He's alive!" ... [The translator] faltered. I repeated the expression several times. Finally, he uttered, *"Avan poikaran."* The Tamils gasped. As I learned afterward, the best he could make of my North Carolina accent was, "He was a liar!"[2]

To help your listeners understand your dialect—or if you speak to people who speak your language as their second language: (1) Use short, simple words. (2) Slow down. Don't talk fast. (3) Pronounce your words clearly. (4) Pause frequently. (5) Repeat your main ideas using different words than you used the first time.

PREACHING TO CHILDREN OR TO A YOUTH GROUP

Children love to participate. They can act out a story, make sound effects, hold props, wear costumes, and repeat words or phrases from the message.[3]

Use simple words and short sentences. Use physical objects (props) to demonstrate ideas. Have them participate with physical movement and verbal response. Be animated and energetic. Use practical examples that come from their own age-group life experiences. Address their fears, worries, hopes, and dreams. Encourage them. Let them know you care about them. Let them know that God loves them. Pray for them.

Note: When speaking to teenagers, sometimes it helps to speak and move faster than you would to a younger or older group. Some youth pastors preach with explosive energy.

PREACHING TO THE ELDERLY

Older people often have hearing loss. It may be hard for them to figure out what you are saying. Loud sounds may hurt their ears. Background noises might blend with your voice, making your words indistinguishable. Older people may think slower, be coping with pain, or have memory problems.

Ways to Modify Your Presentation for Elderly People

Speak at a normal or slower rate. Don't talk fast. Pause often. Pronounce your words clearly. Keep your message short and simple. Use repetition. Rephrase some of your statements using different words. Don't whisper. Don't shout. Don't use drums or clanging instruments. Eliminate extra noise in the room. Speak without musical accompaniment (no piano in the background). Pray for them.

The adaptations suggested in this chapter will help ensure that your ministry efforts are effective. No matter where or to whom you preach, your job remains the same. Let the listeners know you value them, and let them know God loves them. Preach a Scriptural message that meets their needs while you follow the lead of the Holy Spirit.

CHAPTER 34

HOW TO GIVE ALTAR CALLS

I have been on both sides of the altar call experience. There were times when I went down to receive prayer, and God met my needs at the altar. At other times, I have worked on the altar-care ministry team, and God met someone else's needs at the altar.

Some preachers give altar calls. Others don't believe in them. I hope you will give them. Sometimes the altar call is called the "invitation."

The classic altar call invites listeners to come to the altar to receive prayer for:

1. Salvation.
2. Repentance for backsliding and rededication of their lives to Christ.
3. Application of the message to their lives.
4. Any other need.

In the invitation, the preacher offers prayer for the above four areas. He encourages the listeners to lay aside pride or embarrassment and come for God's help.

The altar call is a time of reverent expectation when the persuasiveness of the preaching and the work of the Holy Spirit position the listeners to open their hearts to God. Because the altar call is so important to the Lord, you will hear preachers request that the listeners not get up and leave during the altar call (unless they have an emergency). The altar call is usually given at the end of the service unless the Holy Spirit prompts the preacher to give it at the beginning or in the middle.

TWO TYPES OF ALTAR CALLS

The Advance-Notice Method

In the advance-notice altar call method, the preacher tells the listeners ahead of time about the opportunity to accept Jesus and mentions that *they will be asked to come down to the altar.* Before they raise their hands in response to the invitation, they already know they will be asked to come forward.

You may have heard Billy Graham say something like this: "In a moment, you will have the opportunity to make the most important decision of your life. You will have the opportunity to ask Jesus to come into your heart to be your LORD and to save you from your sin. At that time, *I will be asking you to stand up and come down here to the front.*"

Another example of the advance-notice method might sound like this:

> In a moment, I'm going to pray with everyone who wants to get into right relationship with God. God is a good God. He loves you. Jesus paid the penalty for our sins on the cross. If you ask Him into your heart to save you and be the LORD of your life, He will forgive you, take away your sin, and give you His righteousness. You will become a child of the living God. If you want to be included in this prayer, *raise your hand, stand up, and come down here* to the front right now. Don't be shy. God is not here to shame you. He is here to save you. He loves you. Come.

The Sequential-Response Method

In the sequential-response altar call method, the preacher asks people to raise their hands for prayer (in any of the four areas) *before* they know they will be asked to stand and come down to the altar. *After* the people have raised their hands, the preacher asks them to stand up, then to come down front.

In the following example, the speaker has preached a message on *Forgiveness*:

> Would everyone bow your heads please and close your eyes. No one moving unless you just have to, and no one looking. God loves you so much. He wants you to experience all of His

blessings. He wants to heal your bodies, heal your broken hearts, forgive you of all your sin, fill you with joy, and give you everlasting life in His kingdom.

He sent His Son, Jesus, to shed His blood and suffer on a cross to pay the price for our sins so we could be forgiven. He sent His Son, Jesus, to show us how much He loves us. Jesus said in John 14:6, *"I am the way, the truth, and the life; no man cometh unto the Father, but by me."* In John 3:16 it is written, *"For God so loved the world* [that's you; He loved you so much], *that he gave his only begotten Son, that whosoever believeth in him should not perish, but have everlasting life."*

Right now, you have an opportunity to make a choice—the best choice there is. You can choose life everlasting. If you are sitting here tonight and you know in your heart you are not right with God—if you have never asked Jesus to be your Lord and Savior—God is calling you.

If you do not have a personal relationship with the Lord Jesus and you would like to, *please raise your hand*. Or maybe you asked Jesus into your heart once, but you backslid away from God and have not been living right. And now you know it's time to come home. If that is you, *put up your hand*. And there is a third group of people: you may be struggling to forgive someone, and you would like help with prayer. If that's you, *raise your hand*. And a fourth group: you may need prayer for something else. Maybe it's for family problems, financial problems, health problems, personal problems, or job problems. If you need prayer for any reason, *raise your hand*.

God is in the midst of us, working in our hearts. *If you raised your hand* for any of these four situations, *would you stand up please?* Would everyone in the congregation stand up also? *All of you who raised your hands, come down to the front.* Don't be embarrassed. If you raised your hand or if you should have raised your hand, this is your time. God is here to help you right now. Come down to the front, and we will pray with you. This is your day for a new beginning. Come. We will wait for you.

ADDITIONAL DETAILS

Some preachers ask the congregation to encourage those coming to the altar by praising God or clapping or singing a song together.

Sometimes it helps people to have someone with them when they go down to the altar. You can suggest that family or friends come with the people who raised their hands. Or you can say, "Would all of you turn to the person on your left and your right and ask them if they need to go down to the altar? If they say yes, offer to go down with them. Say, 'I'd be happy to go with you.'"

Once when I asked the lady next to me this question, she said, "Yes. I would like to go, but I can't walk down those stairs without help. And I have my five-year-old granddaughter with me."

I replied, "I would be happy to help you down the stairs. And I'll watch your granddaughter while the prayer partner at the altar prays with you."

Another time five teenage boys were seated behind me. In spite of hearing all his friends say no to my question, the last boy said, "Yes, I want to go down."

I stood up and said, "Come on. I'll go with you." When the prayer partner prayed with him, I stood several feet back so they could talk privately. After we returned from the altar, I said, "I'm so happy you came down for prayer. God bless you."

As he rejoined his friends, he paused, leaned toward me, looked me straight in the eye, and said, "Thank you. Thank you!"

REPEAT-AFTER-ME PRAYERS

When the responders are standing at the altar, you will lead them in a repeat-after-me prayer for salvation, rededication, and application of the message. Speak slowly and clearly in short phrases. Pause with ample time for the listeners to repeat what you said.

SALVATION PRAYERS

Some preachers use short salvation prayers. Others like a longer, more instructive one.

Salvation Prayer Example

Dear Father God, I thank You that You made me and You love me. I want to be in right relationship with You. I thank You that Your Son, Jesus, died on a cross to pay the penalty for my sins. I repent, and I ask You to forgive me of all my sins. I turn away from them.

In the Bible, Romans 10:9 says that if I confess with my mouth that Jesus is Lord, and believe in my heart that God raised Him from the dead, I will be saved. Dear God, I do that now. I confess that Jesus is Lord, and He is my Lord and Savior. I believe in my heart that You raised Him from the dead. Jesus, please come into my heart, be my Lord, and save me. Fill me with Your Holy Spirit.

Father God, Your Word says that whoever calls on the name of the Lord will be saved (Romans 10:13). I have done that, so I thank You that I am saved. I thank You that Jesus took my sin and gave me His righteousness. I now have a reborn spirit and am a born-again Christian. I am Your child and will spend eternity with You. Thank You. I am grateful. In Jesus' name, amen.

Short Salvation Prayer Example

Dear Father God, I repent of my sins, and I ask You to forgive me. I believe in my heart that Jesus is the Son of God who died on a cross, paid for my sins with His blood, and rose from the dead. I confess that Jesus is Lord. Jesus, please come into my heart, be my Lord and Savior, and fill me with Your Holy Spirit. Thank You for saving me. In Jesus' name, amen.

PRAYER FOR APPLICATION OF THE MESSAGE

After the prayer for salvation, you can continue with a repeat-after-me prayer that helps people apply the message. This example is from a message on *Forgiveness*:

> Father, I ask You to help me forgive everyone who has harmed me. You forgave me, and You want me to forgive them. Please heal the hurts inside of me and help me be a forgiving person. By an act of my will, I state that I forgive all who have hurt me. I forgive _____ (now quietly speak the names of the people you are forgiving; no one has to hear these names except God).
>
> Continue to repeat after me: Father, I turn away from unforgiveness. I ask You to forgive me of the bitterness I have held. You said in Matthew 5:44 that I should bless those that curse me and pray for those who despitefully use me and persecute me. Therefore, I pray that You would heal the people who have harmed me so Your will can be done in their lives. I know that because I forgave and prayed for them, Your hand of blessing will be upon me. I thank You. I pray in the name of Jesus, amen.

The preacher will often invite the rest of the congregation to repeat the prayers aloud along with the people who are at the altar. Think about your altar call. Practice it out loud. Also, watch other preachers so you get a feel for the flow of the altar call.

CHAPTER 35

FINISH-UP DETAILS AFTER YOU PREACH

After you leave the church, you may be inclined to go on to the next task or into relaxation mode. But if you take a moment to contemplate your preaching, it will help you learn and grow. I have found that the best time to evaluate and learn from a presentation is very soon after it is completed.

QUESTIONS TO ASK YOURSELF AFTER THE MESSAGE

Write notes to yourself about what worked, what didn't work, and what you would change.

Ask yourself:

1. Did I preach what God wanted me to preach?
2. Did I preach it from my heart—with sincerity, belief, and even passion?
3. Did I use illustrations, examples, stories, metaphors, etc., that the audience could relate to?
4. Did I make the main idea of the message clear?
5. Did I show the audience how to apply the message to their lives?
6. Did I follow the lead of the Holy Spirit?
7. Did I give an altar call?

Think about:

1. Your connection with God during the message.
2. Your connection with the listeners.
3. Your presentation style: voice, body, movements, facial expressions, volume, and timing.
4. Your emotional levels: happiness, peace, anxiety, etc.
5. Your organization of the concepts.
6. If all the concepts were Scriptural or if you got off into opinion.
7. The reception of your message by the audience.
8. The physical technicalities: room set-up, microphone, heating or cooling systems, management by the ushers, etc.
9. Your level of preparation.
10. Communication with the leaders or person who invited you to speak.

Answer these questions:

1. What did I do well?
2. If I could do it over again, what would I change?
3. What did I learn that I can apply the next time?
4. What is my next step?

Write your answers in a preaching-assessment notebook. You can improve by reviewing your suggestions to yourself.

SPIRITUAL AND PHYSICAL COMPLETION ACTIONS

Praise God

Give credit to whom credit is due. That gifting placed in you is from God. Every ability and strength you have came from Him. Thank Him, praise Him, worship Him. Position yourself for God's protection with sincere and loving praise and worship.

Pay Attention

> *Finally, my brethren, be strong in the* Lord, *and in the power of his might. Put on the whole armour of God, that ye may be able to stand against the wiles of the devil.* (Ephesians 6:10–11)

Be ready for a counterattack. It may come in your thoughts or emotions. You may think, *How foolish to think I could preach. Why did I get so intense? I probably scared everyone off. I never want to preach again.*

The enemy may try to frighten, discourage, or confuse you. If your message was successful, be careful. Sometimes after a triumph comes a trial or defeat. When you drive home, be cautious. Drive safely. Pay attention. If you wake up the next morning blanketed with depression, be aware of the enemy's tactics. Fight it off with the Sword of the Spirit (Scripture). Don't let it stay.

Pay attention in the physical realm, thought realm, emotional realm, and spiritual realm.

Write Thank-You Notes

Thank the pastor and the meeting planner for the opportunity to minister. Pray a blessing over them.

If you will practice the completion suggestions, you will learn more fully from each preaching experience. You will also help yourself stay balanced and protected.

SECTION VII

THE LAST CHAPTER

CHAPTER 36

GOD BLESS YOU

You have just finished reading a big, detail-filled book. We covered a lot of ground. It would be easy for you to be overwhelmed and not use the information. Don't yield to that temptation. Do an assessment of your speaking abilities. What are your strengths and weaknesses? In what areas do you need to improve?

Start with the basics and work your way up. For instance, if your pronunciation is difficult for listeners to understand, practice speaking more clearly.

Choose one or two things to work on. When you have incorporated them into your speaking, choose another skill to learn. Don't focus on too many suggestions at once.

Also, don't worry about making a mistake. Don't try to do everything perfectly. I don't want you to think you have to preach in a certain way or that there is only one way to be an effective preacher. There are many ways. The suggestions in this book are not rigid rules, never to be broken. Every now and then, you will see a preacher do the opposite of what I suggest, and it's okay. It even seems to work. There is freedom to be you.

I know of a preacher who always opens with a joke that is not related to his theme. For most preachers, this would not work. But this pastor is very likable, he enjoys it, and it turns out fine.

The following example of departing from traditional message-writing occurred because the preacher understood his main goal:

> One Sunday night at church, Marty Blackwelder, the associate pastor, walked up to the lectern and said something like this: "I've

been praying all week, asking God what He wanted me to preach. The only thing I've gotten is the word *saturate*. I researched *saturate*, but a message did not come. It's my turn to preach, and I don't have a message. But I know my job is to follow the lead of the Holy Spirit. He gave me the word *saturate*, which means to soak or fill to maximum capacity. Let's start singing, and we'll find out what He has in mind."[1]

We began to sing, "You are a mighty God. You are a mighty God. Mighty God." We sang for maybe ten minutes. Then Pastor Marty said a few sentences, but he soon stopped speaking and started singing again because he detected that the Holy Spirit was not leading him to talk. This sequence happened three or four times. He'd start to speak, then pull back and start singing again.

We sang "Mighty God" over and over again. Each time we sang it, the intensity of the worship increased. The presence of God filled the sanctuary. And on and on we sang "Mighty God." It was awesome. It was magnificent. It was exquisite.

Do you see how easy it would have been for this associate pastor to become worried about not having a message? If he had written one and preached it, we all would have missed out on experiencing God's glory. Don't be afraid to "break the rules" in order to follow the lead of the Holy Spirit.

Every book has an ending. But I hope the ending of this book will be a new beginning for you. I hope you will use this book to step up to your next level in your speaking and preaching. Speaking for God is a combination of the natural and supernatural working together—so pray, read your Bible, and prepare.

Always remember: The technical details are not the most important part of preaching (unless no one can figure out what you are saying).

Focus on your top priorities. When you preach, share the wonderful news of God's goodness. Let the listeners know that God loves them. Be authentic. Be sincere. At times, be vulnerable. Share your heart with your listeners. Let them know you care about them. Always be Scriptural. Offer your message up to God as an act of worship, and follow the lead of the Holy Spirit.

As I wrote this book, I saw you all in my mind—young, middle-aged, and old, coming from every race, every nation, every Christian church, every economic and educational level, male and female, answering the call of God to speak for Him.

With deep gratitude to God, I submit this information to you. May you prosper, be in health, and move forward in the ministry to which God has called you. May the fire of God burn in you and the love of God flow through you as you speak His message of reconciliation.

God bless you!
Pam Barnett

So, as much as in me is, I am ready to preach the gospel to you . . . For I am not ashamed of the gospel of Christ: for it is the power of God unto salvation to every one that believeth; to the Jew first, and also to the Greek. (Romans 1:15–16)

NOTES

ACKNOWLEDGMENTS

1. The Ministry Training and Development Institute at Oral Roberts University offered a non-credit, one time a week, one year course in Practical Aspects of Charismatic Ministry, year 2002.

CHAPTER 1: PREACHING BASICS

1. Warren Wiersbe and David Wiersbe, *The Elements of Preaching*. (Wheaton, Illinois: Tyndale House Publishers, 1986), 17.

CHAPTER 2: PREACHING IS A RELATIONSHIP EVENT

1. Kenneth W. Hagin, spoken in a pastoral training class at Rhema Bible Training College, 2001.

CHAPTER 4: HOW TO BUILD CREDIBILITY AS A PREACHER

1. G. Calvin McCutchen, Sr., quoted in "God's Civil Servant" by Tara Lynn Thompson, *Community Spirit*, March 2007, Equipment Publications, Tulsa, Oklahoma, 9.
2. William Evans, *How to Prepare Sermons*. (Chicago: Moody Press, 1964), 18.

CHAPTER 5: GUIDELINES FOR A GUEST SPEAKER OR TRAVELING MINISTER

1. Marvin Yoder, *The Traveling Minister's Handbook*. (Tulsa, Oklahoma: Faith Library Publications, 2000), 181.

CHAPTER 6: THE ANOINTING

1. James Strong, LLD., S.T.D., *The New Strong's Exhaustive Concordance of the Bible*, (Nashville, TN: Thomas Nelson, 1990), 78 Greek Dictionary section.
2. W. E. Vine, Merrill F. Unger, William White Jr., *Vine's Complete Expository Dictionary of Old and New Testament Words*. (Nashville, TN: Thomas Nelson, 1996), 5, Old Testament section.
3. Donald E. Demaray, *Introduction to Homiletics,* Second Edition. (Indianapolis, Indiana: Light and Life Press, 1990), 22.
4. James Strong, LLD., S.T.D., *The New Strong's Exhaustive Concordance of the Bible*, (Nashville, TN: Thomas Nelson, 1990), 78 Greek Dictionary section.
5. W. E. Vine, Merrill F. Unger, William White Jr., *Vine's Complete Expository Dictionary of Old and New Testament Words*. (Nashville, TN: Thomas Nelson, 1996), 28, New Testament section.

6. Charles Haddon Spurgeon, as quoted by John Piper in his internet article "Charles Spurgeon: Preaching Through Adversity," 6, website: www.founders.org/FJ23/article1.html, original source: *An All Round Ministry*, 358.
7. Kenneth Copeland, *From Faith to Faith: A Daily Guide to Victory*. (Tulsa, Oklahoma: Harrison House, 1992), page for November 12.
8. Marvin Yoder, *The Traveling Minister's Handbook*. (Tulsa, Oklahoma: Faith Library Publications, 2000), 214.
9. The Ministry Training and Development Institute at Oral Roberts University offered a non-credit, one-time-a-week, one-year course in Practical Aspects of Charismatic Ministry, year 2002.
10. Frank Hultgren, spoken at Oral Roberts University in a class of The Ministry Training and Development Institute, year 2002.

CHAPTER 7: WHAT IS THE GOSPEL?

1. Bill Bright, *Have You Heard of the Four Spiritual Laws?* (Orlando, Florida: New Life Publications, Campus Crusade for Christ, 2000).
2. Billy Joe Daugherty, church brochures at Victory Christian Center, Tulsa, Oklahoma.
3. LaDonna C. Osborn, *God's Big Picture: Finding Yourself in God's Plan*. (Tulsa, Oklahoma, Osborn Publishers, 2001), 26.
4. Ibid., 42.

CHAPTER 10: FEAR-REDUCTION TECHNIQUES

1. R. T. Kendall, *The Anointing: Yesterday, Today, Tomorrow*. (Lake Mary, Florida: Charisma House, 2003), 115.

CHAPTER 11: HOW TO MANAGE FEAR SYMPTOMS DURING THE MESSAGE

1. Kate McVeigh, spoken in a presentation at Rhema Bible Training College, year 2000.
2. Joan Detz, *How to Write & Give a Speech*, revised edition. (New York, New York: St. Martin's Press, 1992), 140.
3. Ibid., 140–141.

CHAPTER 12: CONFIDENCE AND THE PERCEPTION OF CONFIDENCE

1. John C. Maxwell, *Be a People Person*. (Colorado Springs, Colorado: Chariot Victor Publishing, a division of Cook Communications, 1994), 36.

CHAPTER 13: TAKE CARE OF THE TEMPLE OF GOD

1. Don Colbert, M.D., *The Bible Cure for Stress*. (Lake Mary, Florida: Siloam Press, 2002), vi–vii.
2. Kenneth E. Hagin, spoken in a class at Rhema Bible Training College, year 2001.
3. Billy Graham, *Just As I Am*. (San Francisco: HarperCollins, Zondervan, 1997).
4. David Beebe, teacher at Rhema Bible Training College, spoken in a class, year 2000.

CHAPTER 15: IDENTIFY YOUR HABITS

1. David L. Larsen, *The Anatomy of Preaching: Identifying the Issues in Preaching Today*. (Grand Rapids, Michigan: Kregel, 1989), 192. Used by permission of the publisher. All rights reserved.

CHAPTER 16: PRAYERS BEFORE PREACHING

1. R. A. Torrey, *Why God Used D. L. Moody*. (Minneapolis, Minnesota: World Wide Publications in cooperation with the Billy Graham Institute of Evangelism, 1992), 17.
2. Charles Spurgeon (Compiled by Tom Carter), *Spurgeon at His Best*. (Grand Rapids, Michigan: Baker Book House, 1991), 143.
3. Ibid., 149.
4. Charles Spurgeon, *Lectures to My Students*. (Grand Rapids, Michigan: Baker Book House, 1981), 156.
5. Oswald Chambers, *My Utmost for His Highest*. (Grand Rapids, Michigan: Discovery House Publishers, 1992), page for January 7.
6. R. A. Torrey, *Why God Used D. L. Moody*. (Minneapolis, Minnesota: World Wide Publications in cooperation with the Billy Graham Institute of Evangelism, 1992),18.
7. David L. Larsen, *The Anatomy of Preaching: Identifying the Issues in Preaching Today*. (Grand Rapids, Michigan: Kregel, 1989), 55. Used by permission of the publisher. All rights reserved.
8. Billy Graham, *Just As I Am*. (San Francisco: HarperCollins, Zondervan, 1997), 267.
9. Keith Moore, spoken while running a Healing School class at Rhema Bible Training College, 2001.

CHAPTER 17: FOLLOW BASIC MESSAGE GUIDELINES

1. R. A. Torrey, *Why God Used D. L. Moody*. (Minneapolis, Minnesota: World Wide Publications in cooperation with the Billy Graham Institute of Evangelism, 1992), 27–28.
2. Charles Spurgeon, *Spurgeon at His Best*. (Grand Rapids, Michigan: Baker Book House, 1988), page 156: #1054, page 159: #1078.
3. David L. Larsen, *The Anatomy of Preaching: Identifying the Issues in Preaching Today*. (Grand Rapids, Michigan): Kregel, 1989, 102. Used by permission of the publisher. All rights reserved.

CHAPTER 18: CHOOSE THE MESSAGE

1. Doug Jones, teacher at Rhema Bible Training College, spoken in a class, year 2000.
2. Mark Sutton, "At Gunpoint," *Leadership* magazine. (Carol Stream, Illinois: Christianity Today International, Fall 2006, Vol. XXVII Number 4), 63.
3. Billy Joe Watts, teacher at Rhema Bible Training College, spoken in a preaching class, year 2000.
4. Kenneth W. Hagin, pastor of Rhema Bible Church, spoken in a class at Rhema Bible Training College, year 2001.
5. Billy Joe Watts, teacher at Rhema Bible Training College, spoken in a preaching class, year 2001.
6. Bill Bush, teacher at Rhema Bible Training College, spoken in a preaching class, year 2001.
7. Michael J. Hostetler, *Introducing the Sermon: The Art of Compelling Beginnings*. (Grand Rapids, Michigan, Ministry Resources Library, Zondervan Publishing House, 1986), 13.

CHAPTER 19: ORGANIZE THE MESSAGE: PART I

1. Nathaniel M. Van Cleave, *Handbook of Preaching*. (San Dimas, California: L.I.F.E. Bible College, 1943, Revised edition 1983), 81.
2. John A. Broadus, *On the Preparation and Delivery of Sermons* Fourth Edition, Revised by Vernon L. Stanfield. (New York, New York: Harper San Francisco, 1979), 129.
3. James Braga, *How to Prepare Bible Messages*. (Portland, Oregon: Multnomah Publishers, Inc., 1981), 233.

CHAPTER 21: CHOOSE THE RIGHT WORDS: GENERAL GUIDELINES

1. *Webster's New World Dictionary*. (New York, New York: POCKET BOOKS, a division of Simon & Schuster Inc., 1995), 522, 314.
2. Billy Joe Daugherty, spoken in a message at Victory Christian Center, Tulsa, Oklahoma, year 2005.

CHAPTER 22: USE IMAGERY TO ANCHOR A CONCEPT

1. Billy Joe Daugherty, spoken in messages presented at Victory Christian Center, Tulsa, Oklahoma, year 2006.
2. Henrietta C. Mears, *What the Bible Is All About*. (Ventura, California: Regal Books a Division of Gospel Light, NIV edition 1998), 449.
3. John C. Maxwell, *The Power of Thinking Big*. (Tulsa, Oklahoma: RiverOak Publishing, 2001), 88.
4. James C. Humes, *The Sir Winston Method: The Five Secrets of Speaking the Language of Leadership*. (New York: William Morrow and Company, Inc., 1991), 67.
5. Joel Osteen, pastor of Lakewood Church, Houston, Texas, spoken in a televised message on TBN.
6. Joyce Meyer, *Celebration of Simplicity: Loving God and Enjoying Life*. (New York, New York: Warner Books, Inc., 2001), 81.

CHAPTER 23: CREATE MEMORABLE WORDING

1. Rick Warren, *The Purpose Driven Life*. (Grand Rapids, Michigan: Zondervan, 2002), 124.
2. Anne Stilman, *Grammatically Correct*. (Cincinnati, Ohio: Writer's Digest Books, 1997), 223.
3. John C. Maxwell, *The Power of Thinking Big*. (Tulsa, Oklahoma: RiverOak Publishing, 2001), 91.
4. Ibid., 86.
5. Derric Johnson, *Excellence Is Never an Accident*. (Tulsa, Oklahoma: Trade Life Books, 1997), 91.
6. Rick Warren, *The Purpose Driven Life*. (Grand Rapids, Michigan: Zondervan, 2002), 91.

CHAPTER 26: HOW TO PRACTICE DELIVERY OF THE MESSAGE

1. Billy Graham, *Just As I Am*. (San Francisco: HarperCollins and Zondervan, 1997), 49.
2. Delivering the Message: Introduction
3. Warren Wiersbe and David Wiersbe, *The Elements of Preaching*. (Carol Stream, Illinois: Tyndale House, 1986), 91.
4. Jack Hughes, *Expository Preaching with Word Pictures*. (Scotland: Christian Focus Publications, 2001), 10.

CHAPTER 33: PRESENTATION MODIFICATIONS FOR SPECIFIC GROUPS

1. Billy Graham, *Just As I Am*. (San Francisco: HarperCollins and Zondervan, 1997), 64.
2. Ibid., 267.
3. Beth Edington Hewitt, *Captivating Children's Sermons*. (Grand Rapids, Michigan: Baker Books, 2005), 38.

CHAPTER 37: GOD BLESS YOU

1. Marty Blackwelder, Associate pastor at Rhema Bible Church, Broken Arrow, Oklahoma, spoken in a worship service, year 2001.

SELECTED BIBLIOGRAPHY

Anderson, Robert C. *The Effective Pastor: A Practical Guide to the Ministry*. Chicago: Moody Press, 1985.

Beatty, Christopher. *Vocal Workout*. Nashville, Tennessee: Star Song Publishing Group, 1992.

Beatty, Christopher. *Maximum Vocal Performance*. Nashville, Tennessee: Star Song Publishing Group, 1992.

Braga, James. *How to Prepare Bible Messages*. Portland, Oregon: Multnomah Publishers, 1981.

Broadus, John A. *On the Preparation and Delivery of Sermons*, Fourth Edition, Revised by Vernon L. Stanfield. San Francisco: HarperCollins, 1979.

Colbert, Don, M.D., *The Bible Cure for Stress*. Lake Mary, Florida: Siloam Press, 2002.

Cooper, Morton. *Change Your Voice Change Your Life*. Los Angeles: Voice and Speech Company of America, (1984 Macmillan Publishing Company), 1999.

Cooper, Morton. *Winning With Your Voice: 5 Minutes a Day to a More Effective Winning Voice*. Los Angeles: Voice and Speech Company of America, 1990.

Copeland, Kenneth. *From Faith to Faith: A Daily Guide to Victory*. Tulsa, Oklahoma: Harrison House, 1992.

Daugherty, Billy Joe. *Led by the Spirit: How God Guides and Provides*. Lake Mary, Florida: Creation House: Strang Communications Company, 1994.

Demaray, Donald E. *An Introduction to Homiletics* Second Edition. Indianapolis, Indiana: Light and Life Press, 1990.

Detz, Joan. *How to Write and Give a Speech.* New York: St. Martin's Press, 1992.

Detz, Joan. *Can You Say a Few Words?* New York: St. Martin's Press, 1991.

Evans, William. *How to Prepare Sermons.* Chicago: Moody, 1964.

Garlock, John. *Keys to Better Preaching.* Tulsa, Oklahoma: Faith Library Publications, 2000.

Graham, Billy. *Just As I Am.* San Francisco: HarperCollins, Zondervan, 1997.

Hagin, Kenneth E. *How You Can Be Led by the Spirit of God.* Tulsa, Oklahoma: Faith Library Publications, 1986.

Henrichsen, Walter A. *A Layman's Guide to Interpreting the Bible.* Grand Rapids, Michigan: Lamplighter Books, Zondervan Publishing House, (1978 by The Navigators), 1985.

Hewitt, Beth Edington. *Captivating Children's Sermons.* Grand Rapids, Michigan: Baker Books, 2005.

Hinn, Benny. *The Anointing.* Nashville, Tennessee: Thomas Nelson Publishers, 1997.

Hostetler, Michael J. *Introducing the Sermon: The Art of Compelling Beginnings.* Grand Rapids, Michigan: Ministry Resources Library, an imprint of Zondervan, 1986.

Hughes, Jack. *Expository Preaching with Word Pictures.* Scotland: Christian Focus Publications, 2001.

Humes, James C. *The Sir Winston Method: The Five Secrets of Speaking the Language of Leadership.* New York: William Morrow and Company, 1991.

Humes, James C. *Standing Ovation: How to Be an Effective Speaker and Communicator.* New York, New York: Harper & Row, Publishers, 1988.

Kendall, R.T. *The Anointing: Yesterday, Today, Tomorrow.* Lake Mary, Florida: Charisma House, Strang, 2003.

Kushner, Malcolm. *Public Speaking for Dummies.* Foster City, California: IDG Books Worldwide, Inc., 1999.

Larsen, David L. *The Anatomy of Preaching: Identifying the Issues in Preaching Today.* Grand Rapids, Michigan: Kregel Publications, 1999.

Lawson, Terry. *How to Study the Word: Taking the Bible from the Pages to the Heart.* Tulsa, Oklahoma: Faith Library Publications, 1999.

Malmin, Ken. *Bible Research* Revised Edition. Portland, Oregon: City Bible Publishing, 1990.

Maxwell, John C. *Be a People Person.* Colorado Springs, Colorado: Chariot Victor Publishing, 1994.

Maxwell, John C. *The Power of Thinking Big*. Tulsa, Oklahoma: RiverOak Publishing, 2001.

Mears, Henrietta C. *What the Bible Is All About* NIV Edition. Ventura, California: Regal Books, 1998.

Mickelsen, A. Berkeley & Mickelsen, Alvera M. *Understanding Scripture: How to Read and Study the Bible*. Peabody, Massachusetts: Hendrickson Publishers Inc., 1992.

Osborn, LaDonna C. *God's Big Picture: Finding Yourself in God's Plan*. Tulsa, Oklahoma: Osborn Publishers, 2001.

Sproul, R.C. *Knowing Scripture*. Downers Grove, Illinois: InterVarsity Press, 1977.

Spurgeon, Charles H. *Lectures to My Students: A Selection from Addresses Delivered to the Students of The Pastors' College, Metropolitan Tabernacle*. Grand Rapids, Michigan: Baker, 1977.

Spurgeon, Charles H. *Spurgeon at His Best* compiled by Tom Carter. Grand Rapids, Michigan: Baker, 1988.

Strong, James, LLD., S.T.D., *The New Strong's Exhaustive Concordance of the Bible*. Nashville, Tennessee: Thomas Nelson, 1990.

Torrey, R. A. *Why God Used D. L. Moody*. Minneapolis, Minnesota: World Wide Publications in cooperation with the Billy Graham Institute of Evangelism, 1992.

Van Cleave, Nathaniel M. *Handbook of Preaching*. San Dimas, California: L.I.F.E. Bible College, 1983.

Vine, W. E., and Unger, Merrill F., and White Jr., William. *Vine's Complete Expository Dictionary of Old and New Testament Words*. Nashville, Tennessee: Thomas Nelson, 1996.

Vines, Jerry and Shaddix, Jim. *Power in the Pulpit*. Chicago: Moody, 1999.

Warren, Rick. *The Purpose Driven Life*. Grand Rapids, Michigan: Zondervan, 2002.

Wiersbe, Warren and Wiersbe, David. *The Elements of Preaching*. Wheaton, Illinois: Tyndale House Publishers, 1986.

Yoder, Marvin. *The Traveling Minister's Handbook* (second edition). Tulsa, Oklahoma: Faith Library Publications, 2000.

ABOUT THE AUTHOR

Pam Barnett is a Christian communication and public-speaking coach. She works with preachers, student preachers, and Christian speakers who want to step up to their own next level as a Holy Spirit-led speaker for God.

She has been a seminar leader, member of the National Speakers Association, results coach, teacher, and speech pathologist. She holds a Bachelor of Arts degree from San Jose State University and four teaching credentials. She is also a graduate of Rhema Bible Training College, where she trained as a pastor.

Pam is gifted in her ability to see both the big picture and the supporting details of a topic. She excels at breaking subject matter down into small, teachable units. No matter what her career titles have been, she has always done three things: teach, coach, and encourage.

Her web site is: SpeakingForGod.com

Email: speakingforgod@cfaith.com

NOTE TO THE READER

Dear Friend,

If you like this book, would you help spread the word by doing these things?

- Write a review on Amazon.com and barnesandnoble.com.
- Tell your friends and pastors about this book.
- Ask your local library to order it. When it arrives, check it out.
- Recommend it to your Bible school or seminary.
- Give it away as a gift.
- Send me an email at speakingforgod@cfaith.com telling me how you feel about this book, what parts you liked best, or stories of how it has helped you.

Thank you!
Pam Barnett

PRAYER FOR A PERSONAL RELATIONSHIP WITH THE LORD

The most glorious thing that can happen to any person is to have a personal relationship with God through His Son, Jesus Christ.

If you want to be in right standing with God, be forgiven of your sins, receive the Holy Spirit on the inside of you, and receive everlasting life, sincerely pray aloud a prayer like this:

> Dear Father God,
>
> I thank You that You made me and You love me. I repent of my sins.
>
> I believe in my heart that Jesus is the Son of God. I believe He died on a cross, paid for my sins with His blood, and rose from the dead. Jesus, come into my heart and be my Lord and Savior. Please forgive me of my sins and fill me with Your Holy Spirit.
>
> I confess that Jesus is Lord, and He is my Lord. Father, I thank You that I am now cleansed, my spirit is reborn, and I will spend eternity with You.
>
> Romans 10:13 says that whoever calls on the name of the Lord shall be saved. Lord, I have called on Your name, so I thank You now for saving me and making me new. I am very grateful. Amen.

If you have just prayed this prayer for the first time, the Bible says God has delivered you from the power of darkness and has transferred you into the kingdom of His dear Son, in whom you have redemption through His blood, the forgiveness of sins (Colossians 1:13–15). Hurray!

This is the beginning of a wonderful relationship for you with God. You can develop your relationship with Him by doing the following: (1) Pray regularly. (2) Get a Bible and read it. A good place to start is with the book of Matthew in the New Testament. (3) Attend a Bible-believing church.

Welcome into the family of God!

www.ingramcontent.com/pod-product-compliance
Lightning Source LLC
Chambersburg PA
CBHW072048110526
44590CB00018B/3078